CW00573446

your essential
guide to what's
hip & happening

Cool!

Bang|kok

Greg Lowe

Marshall Cavendish
Editions

Author's Note

Bangkok has always been an easy place to have fun in. For years it has enjoyed fame and infamy as a 24-hour, anything-goes party city, but as with most stereotypes, this reputation is only in part true and the city's hedonistic wings have been clipped to some extent over the past decade.

That being said, you'd have to be practically certifiable to be bored in a city which was named World's Best City in 2008 and 2010 by Travel + Leisure magazine, thanks to a groundswell in its offering of shops, clubs, bars, restaurants and spas.

Any issues with Bangkok's shopping, culinary or nightlife scenes have little to do with a lack of choice; the real problem is knowing how to navigate this chaotic Asian metropolis and seek out the notable shops, bars, hotels and restaurants from the thousands of venues scattered around the city. Cool Bangkok! aims to make this experience easier by indentifying local establishments that stand out from the maddening homogenous crowd and, where possible, grouping them by activity and geographic location.

While Thailand's capital is not a world city like London or New York, what it lacks in cosmopolitanism it makes up for with passion and raw energy, unashamedly wearing its developing world attitude on its sleeve.

Its rugged cityscape is home to ghost buildings left derelict since the 1997 Asian financial crisis that overlook luxury residential developments and historic centres. Urban sprawl and bad traffic hide pockets of cool where clusters of shops, bars and restaurants cater to a leftfield crowd. It is a place where Michelin-starred chefs and city boys chow down on 30-baht bowls of noodles alongside street hawkers and itinerant workers, and high-society kids rub shoulders with local rock stars and indie kids in the same bar.

When writing Cool Bangkok!, care was taken to focus predominantly on locally-owned standalone businesses that are distinct for their imagination and creativity and for having clear identity and personality. Thai chains were only included if they were exceptional and pioneers in their respective fields, such as Greyhound and Kloset in the shopping section. The only international brands to earn a place in the book were nahm, Sra Bua by Kiin Kiin and Face; restaurants and bars that are truly world-class.

Lastly, there are many places worth visiting that have not been included because of space. Bangkok is in a constant state of flux with new places opening and closing on a daily basis. While the venues listed in this book do stand out for their individualism and are likely to keep pushing the boundaries for years to come, some will undoubtedly fall by the wayside as new establishments continue to raise the bar.

The best way to experience Bangkok as a city that stimulates all the senses is to throw caution to the wind and jump in the deep end. Hopefully this guide will help you swim that little bit better.

Greg Lowe
August 2011

LOCALES

If Bangkok has a centre point it's **SIAM SQUARE**, where the intersection of the BTS skytrain's Silom and Sukhumvit lines make for a natural stop-off point. Plus there are literally hundreds of stores, stalls, cafes and restaurants crammed into the "square" itself. Walk a few hundred metres and you'll find Siam Center – home to mob F, a floor of Thai fashion brands – while you have the more upscale Siam Discovery on one side and the massive luxury Siam Paragon mall on the other.

A little further down Rama I Road and you come to **RATCHAPRASONG** intersection, the epicentre of boutique malls such as Erawan, Gaysorn Plaza and Peninsula Plaza, with the world's third largest shopping centre, CentralWorld, across the road and Amarin Plaza, which is home to id1, nearby.

SUKHUMVIT ROAD is the longest road in Thailand and it runs from central Bangkok to the Cambodian border. Fortunately, you don't need to travel its entire length in search of a decent party or a place to shop. While it's worth investigating the numerous sois (sidestreets), there are some key places to check out: for food head to Soi Arab and Soi 36, and if you have partying on your mind go to Soi 11, Thong Lor and Ekamai.

SUKHUMVIT SOI 11 is a key nightlife and clubbing destination – several bars and restaurants are found down this little side street. A good place to start a night out is at Cheap Charlies, and you can head for a rooftop sundowner or two at Nest before moving on to Q Bar or Bed Supperclub to boogie.

Over the past few years the number of bars and clubs located on Soi **THONG LOR** has rocketed, in part thanks to the construction of a number of upscale condominiums which have drawn an increasing number of wealthy younger Thais into the area. Community malls and smaller developments such as Grass, J Avenue, Penny's Balcony and Seenspace continue the upscale vibe in this hi-so partyland. Stepping out in this area can be much fun, but be warned, it is not cheap.

EKAMAI, which runs parallel with Thong Lor, is more about eating and drinking, although the Park Lane mall provides some interesting shopping opportunities. While the people who live down the road are no less affluent than those on Thong Lor, Ekamai certainly has a more laidback and less glitzy feel to its bars, so you can enjoy a more down to earth and noticeably cheaper time out at places such as Happy Monday, Bangkok Bar and Pedalicious.

SILOM ROAD is all about eating and drinking. While quality shopping is hard to find, hedonism and bacchanalia are never more than a stone's throw away. A top place to start a sleaze-free night out is Silom Soi 4.

Out & About

DON'T WORRY IF YOU'VE TICKED ALL THE BOXES ON YOUR CHECKLIST OF PLACES TO FEAST, SHOP AND PARTY, OR IF YOU'VE HAD YOUR CAFFEINE FIX BUT ARE STILL IN SEARCH OF SOMETHING MORE RELAXING TO DO. BANGKOK NOT ONLY ROCKS, IT RELAXES TOO AND PERHAPS ONE OF THE FIRST LOW-KEY ACTIVITIES TO INDULGE IN IS A FOOT MASSAGE OR SPA TREATMENT, AFTER WHICH YOU CAN PAD AROUND A LOCAL GALLERY EXHIBITING CUTTING EDGE PHOTOGRAPHY AND VISUAL ART, OR CATCH A FLICK AT SCALA, ONE OF THE GRAND DAMES OF THE SOUTHEAST ASIAN CINEMA CIRCUIT.

RELAX

Step back in time

For a personalised and authentic Thai massage take a trip to Spa at Face, which is set amongst some of the city's most oasis-like surrounds.

It's almost impossible not to completely relax as soon as you enter the traditional-style teak sala. The air is infused with aromatic oils from incense burners and the dark teak wood surrounds and subdued lighting have their own curative influences.

An extensive range of spa therapies, including Thai herbal steam treatments, skin scrubs and aromatherapy massages, are on offer from expertly trained masseuses. But given the bespoke nature of the small spa and the stunning surrounds, you do pay a premium price at Face. The indulgence, however, is definitely worth it.

Spa at Face Sukhumvit Soi 38
Tel: 02-713 6048 www.facebars.com

Reflex Action

Foot Master is one of the few places in Bangkok that specialises in Chinese reflexology and its different technique, chic environment and consistent quality of treatments sets it apart from most places that offer the ubiquitous Thai foot massage.

Dark terracotta walls, water features and bamboo create a relaxed, soothing environment. The massages are conducted in huge, super-comfy reclining seats (each one has an arm-mounted TV complete with headphones) and the experience is further enhanced with the use of a heated, aromatic neck cushion which amplifies the relaxed bliss.

As the Chinese massage relies more on acupressure techniques than the kneading and stretching on which Thai massage is based, it can be a more painful experience. But it is worth grinning and bearing the intensity as the relief that comes after the tension and knots have been forced into submission is always worth it.

Foot Master also offers body massage and a number of specialist foot treatments – there's even reflexology for kids. The standard 45-minute reflexology massage costs 300 baht.

Foot Master 3F Amarin Plaza, Ploenchit Road
Tel: 02-684 1506

Panpuri Organic Spa

Time seems to slow as soon as you walk into the Panpuri Organic spa; relaxing music and aromatic scents sooth the senses, an experience which becomes all the more consuming when you enter the treatment rooms.

While the wellness centre is a spinoff from Panpuri, one of Thailand's leading purveyors of spa and aromatherapy products, it has avoided making the typical nods to traditional Thai design and architecture which have become a trademark of the kingdom's hospitality industry. Instead there's a contemporary, Asian-inspired approach to the design: diffusely-lit rooms are walled in black ceramic tiles with a smattering of gold mosaic. The end result is a distinctly subdued, wound-down vibe which add to the delight of disconnecting from the hustle and bustle of Bangkok's streets that are a mere stone's throw away.

In terms of treatments, beyond the use of organic-only oils and products, the spa offers a range of Thai and Asian massage and spa therapies, as well as scrubs, baths and packages for individuals and couples. While the menu may not be as extensive as at other spas, this means it lacks a lot of the fads and more ridiculous treatments that have become commonplace and therapists are left to concentrate on providing superlative levels of service. Expect to pay upwards of 2,000 baht for a package.

Panpuri Organic Spa Gaysorn Plaza, Ratchaprasong
Tel: 02-656 1199 www.panpuriorganicspa.com

ART

Social Space

Libraries are rarely seen as centres of cool, but Narawan Pathomvat has re-engineered the traditional bibliotheque and refashioned it into a social space that is a centre for students, artists and culture vultures.

The Reading Room is a welcoming and informal space with a collection of books which mostly cover art, art history, philosophy and culture in both English and Thai. But it's the events, such as discussions, book readings and film screenings, which catalyse passionate debates that make the place so engaging.

"The events that we host make the space very active and energetic which I think is very distinctive and rare in comparison to other libraries," says Narawan.

The Reading Room 2 Silom Soi 19
Tel: 02-635 3674 www.readingroombkk.org
Open Wednesday to Sunday

Screen Burn

If you fancy catching a flick while in Bangkok, there are two cinemas that you simply must visit. Scala is the grande dame of Bangkok's movie houses – this single screen cinema was built in 1967 and can pack in some 900 film buffs. As part of the Apex group of cinemas, Scala shows a mix of independent films and major releases, though it is generally discerning in its choice. There are so few places left like this in the world that any self-respecting cinephile would leave Thailand an incomplete person if they failed to at least wander through the lobby of this remnant from the lost era of the Silver Screen.

House RCA is a more recent arrival to the cinematic scene, one which signified a quantum leap in terms of programming. It's fiercely independent and shows Asian and international art house and independent productions as well as more mass market, edgy films such as *Sex and Zen 3D*. It also has a DVD rental library so you can continue your fanboy fanatics at home.

Kathmandu

See another world through photographs at Kathmandu Gallery, a place Manit Sriwanichpoom has said was "born to promote photography". A portrait photographer who gained fame for his Pink Man series, Manit's work typically has a strong social and political context and as such he has struggled to find a place to show exhibit his photography.

At Kathmandu, serious efforts have been made to prevent the gallery from being a stereotypical "white cube", opting instead for a homely approach which uses the first floor to exhibit Manit's work, with a space on the second floor dedicated to local and international photographers. The gallery features both established names and newbies, whose work "must have ideas on how he/she looks at the world". According to the owner, they "try to avoid showing plain travel photos. Photographs have to convey some messages or thoughts."

Kathmandu Photo Gallery 87 Pan Road, off Silom Road
Tel: 02-234 6700

Serindia Gallery

For Shane Suvikapakornkul, opening Serindia Gallery was a natural progression after two decades of publishing high quality art and photography books under his Serindia Publications imprint.

Located in a post-colonial home, the gallery – which takes its name from the Silk Road between China and India – often exhibits works featured in his books. The exhibitions of oil and watercolour paintings, photography and woodcuts are always thematic, "telling interesting stories about the subject, the art, the technique".

While it is essentially a commercial space, quality and taste are paramount as Shane says, "I don't show things I would be embarrassed to have at home myself".

Serindia Gallery OP Garden, Soi Charoen Krung 36
Tel: 02-238 6410 Website: www.serindiagallery.com

Stephff's Gallery

When he's not spending his time entertaining readers of *The Nation* with his political satire, illustrator Stephan Paray – aka Stephff – pursues his other passion of collecting tribal art.

The gallery is a private, appointment-only space, but you get shown around by the man himself who personally assures the authenticity of the pieces. It's a great place to find a bargain, thanks in part the Stephff's low commission and there's a range of figures, carvings and masks from Africa, Asia and Oceania.

He defines tribal art as works which were "not made for sale but for tribal use" and these sell for as little as 5,000 baht to several hundred thousand, with most pieces fetching between 30,000 to 60,000 baht. He also sells contemporary painting, including his own illustrations.

Stephff's Gallery Narathiwat Soi 22
Tel: 02-674 1838 Website: www.stephffgallery.com

TCDC

Fans of design should head to Thailand Creative & Design Center, which is the country's only design resource and exhibition centre, conveniently located on the top of the Emporium mall. The permanent *What is Design?* exhibition features iconic products from 10 countries, but more often than not it is the temporary shows which are more interesting. Some of these are local, but they have included bigger exhibitions ranging from the *DNA of Japanese Design* to the likes of punk provocateur Vivienne Westwood.

TCDC 6F Emporium, Sukhumvit Road
Tel: 02-664 8448 Website: www.tcdc.or.th

BIKING

Eat, Pedal, Drink

Okay, Bangkok's not the world's most cyclist-friendly city, but you may be surprised by the number of people who are opting for pedal power, at least as a leisure pursuit if not for their main mode of transport.

Now that Pedalicious has freewheeled into the world, there's a place for such velocentric types to hang out. Hidden down a side street off Soi Ekamai, the venue combines a bike store, workshop, bar and restaurant all under the same roof, but best of all it's a place to hang out and chat about bikes.

It's a friendly environment and you won't feel out of place even if you don't like cycling. But if you're after a ride the cycles here cost from 10,000 to 20,000 baht as the owners want the prices to be accessible. They also arrange regular bike trips on Saturdays which anyone can join, just call first to check out the route.

Pedalicious Bike & Bistro Ekamai Soi 12
Tel: 02-713 3377 Website: www.facebook.com/Pedalicious
Closed Mondays

Dining

BANGKOK HAS ALWAYS BEEN HOME TO SOME OF THE BEST CUISINES IN THE WORLD. A STROLL DOWN ANY OF THE CITY'S STREETS REVEALS A VAST ARRAY OF FLAVOURS AND INFLUENCES, FROM THE FIERY SPICY ISAAN FOOD OF THE NORTHEAST TO THE MORE AROMATIC SOUTHERN CURRIES AND PLENTY OF OTHER REGIONAL SPECIALITIES IN BETWEEN.

ALTHOUGH THERE HAS ALWAYS BEEN A DECENT RANGE OF OTHER WORLD CUISINES ON OFFER, BANGKOK'S DINING SCENE HAS UNDERGONE SOMETHING OF A REVOLUTION IN RECENT TIMES. IN PARTICULAR, THE CITY HAS SEEN A SURGE IN THE NUMBER OF CHEF-DRIVEN RESTAURANTS THAT HAVE BUILT THEIR REPUTATIONS ON IMAGINATIVE, ORIGINAL CUISINE. TASTING MENUS HAVE BECOME MORE PROMINENT, AS HAS THE EXPERIMENTALISM OF SOUS VIDE AND MOLECULAR GASTRONOMY, FOR WANT OF A BETTER WORD. THIS STEP CHANGE HAS CATALYSED THAI, ASIAN AND WESTERN RESTAURATEURS TO CAST OFF THE SHACKLES OF THEIR VARIOUS TRADITIONS AND ADOPT A MORE PROGRESSIVE APPROACH TO THE ART OF COOKING.

SO WHETHER YOU WANT TO EAT LIKE THE LOCALS, FEAST ON SPANISH, MEXICAN OR FRENCH FARE, OR PUSH THE BOAT OUT AND TREAT YOURSELF TO A THAI OR INDIAN MEAL OF NEAR MICHELIN-STAR QUALITY, BANGKOK PUNCHES WELL ABOVE ITS WEIGHT AS A FOODIE'S HEAVEN.

Bento Boom

While Edoya has been a hit with the local Japanese community for more than three decades, it still hasn't registered on many people's radar. The traditional restaurant serves an extensive range of sashimi, sushi, okonomiyaki, ramen, yakiniku and more. You can sit at the sashimi bar and watch the chefs at work, pick a table or opt for a private room upstairs.

While the a la carte menu includes a wide range of imported fish and other specialities, it's the lunch sets, which start at less than 200 baht for simple sashimi up to 350 baht for a full-sized bento, that are the key attraction.

Edoya Charn Isara Tower, Rama 4 Road
Tel: 02-233 6141

Rustic Italian

There's a running joke that Bangkok has more Italian restaurants than Italian expats, and the ubiquitous nature of the pizzeria means that quality is highly variable. The typical choice lies between a plethora of joints knocking out pizzas and pastas that have been sweetened and spiced for a Thai palette, or high-end and overpriced bistros claiming the nearest thing to mama's own cooking.

But for a robust range of rustic dishes it's hard to outdo Lido. The food isn't fancy as the chef focuses on perfecting simple, traditional flavours using prime ingredients which win out over maximalist or overly rich sauces. The range of pizzas, pastas and risottos and other specialities is extensive. While there are better Italian joints in Bangkok, you'd be hard-pressed to find one with such a strong combination of quality and value. Lido is also perfectly located for a good meal before heading round the corner to Wong's Place (see p150).

Lido 34/3 Soi Sribmphen, Rama IV Road
Tel: 02-677 6351

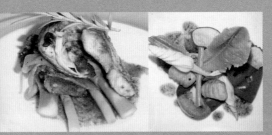

Inspiration Francaise

With the recent proliferation of chef-driven restaurants in Bangkok, it's good to see a relatively young Thai standing his own ground. At La Table de Tee, chef Tee Kachorklin takes his own approach to Thai cuisine. Having cut his teeth working in a Michelin-starred French restaurant in London for four years, followed by a stint at a luxury hotel on the Isle of Wight in England, the 24-year-old returned to Bangkok full of ideas.

Located down a small side street, the restaurant is simply decorated and has enough space for about 18 people. The seven-course tasting menu (which costs 900 baht) is changed more than once a week and the cuisine draws on French and Thai inspirations. Tee is keen to distance himself from the fusion movement, noting that he is a Thai chef who loves French food and is more concerned with creating his own dishes than pigeonholing them.

There's a great subtlety to the flavours and each dish tends to owe more allegiance to one cuisine or the other. The light duck consommé infused with lemon balm, spider crab and egg curd bamboo clarification tips its hat to France, whereas Tee's slowly-cooked glazed pork belly and mini ribs served with a crushed lime dressing is a much more Thai creation.

La Table de Tee Saladaeng Road
Tel: 02-636 3220 Website: www.latabledetee.com

Banoffee Bliss

Despite having room for more than 100 people, The Anna Restaurant's layout always ensures an intimate dining experience. The 100-year-old building features a number of individually designed and decorated rooms with additional seating along a glazed corridor.

"Charlie" Chananudech, who returned to Thailand after a 16-year stint in San Francisco, has designed an extensive mainly-Thai menu, although there are quite a few international dishes, such as Italian pastas, rib-eye steaks and the delectable Casablanca lamb, which is slow-cooked to a succulent, spiced perfection and served with roti.

Whatever main course you opt for, be sure to leave room for pudding. The Anna is famous for its dessert list, the undisputed queen of which is the homemade Banoffee Pie, which is among the best on offer in Bangkok. The crunchy, crumbly biscuit base is topped with dark banoffee, slices of banana and lashings of fresh whipped cream. The tragedy of its popularity is that it's often sold out before the end of lunch.

After eating, you can burn of some of the excess calories by strolling around the art gallery upstairs, which hosts exhibitions by leading local artists and photographers.

The Anna Restaurant 27 Soi Piphat
Tel: 02-237 2788 Website: www.theannarestaurant.com

Café Ice

This lovingly-restored wooden shop house harks back to the Thai Renaissance era and the different rooms with exposed wooden floors have been decked out with a range of European and Asian antiques. There's a touch of art deco to the place but the different styles and aesthetics have been tastefully balanced. Head upstairs to the art gallery if you fancy whetting your cultural appetite before exploring the predominantly Thai menu, which also features a number of French and Italian classics. The portions are massive so it's a great place to share.

Café Ice 44/2 Soi Piphat 2
Tel: 02-636 7272 Website: www.cafeicethailand.com

Sam's Fish & Chips

It's best to negotiate the spiral cast-iron staircase that leads to Sam's Fish & Chips when you haven't had too many drinks and when it's not raining. That goes double when making your descent as you'll most likely have sunk a few cold ones with the affable owner himself.

To describe Sam as friendly is an understatement; he does everything he can to make you feel at home in the leafy rooftop restaurant that serves the best fish and chips in town. The homely feel at Sam's owes a lot to the fact that it is actually his home. He was sitting on the roof having a glass of wine sometime in 2010 while enjoying his wife's gardening, when he thought opening a bar would be a good way to spend his retirement.

The John Dory is fried to perfection and served with proper chunky chips all for 139 baht. There's beer and a limited choice of wine on offer, but beyond the seriously good value and the oasis-like surrounds, the charm is what will keep you coming back.

Sam's Fish & Chips 146 Phiphat Soi 2
Tel: 02-234 73335

Delicious Homemade
European-Western-Thai Foods

nahm

David Thompson broke ground when he opened nahm at the Metropolitan Hotel in London, for it was to become the first Thai restaurant in the world to receive a Michelin Star. In 2010, he returned to his source of inspiration and opened a branch in Bangkok.

The swank restaurant features subdued lighting, dark wooden tables and wood and brick pillars, bolstered by Como Hotels' worldclass service. While the food is presented in a contemporary manner, the flavours are authentic. David spent years researching traditional Thai recipes and has access to the palace archives, enabling him to bring back or re-engineer century-old classics. There's not too much deconstruction applied to the food and the staff will let you know how to eat the more challenging dishes. Moreover, there's no compromise in terms of the flavours or levels of spiciness and a selection of regional dishes is included on each menu which expertly balances the four elements of Thai cuisine – sweet, salt, sour and spice.

The best way to experience nahm is to order the testing menu at 1,700 baht a head.

nahm Metropolitan Hotel, Sathorn Road
Tel: 02-625 3388 Website: www.metropolitan.bangkok.como.bz

RESTAURANTS
Sukhumvit Road

Antique Oasis

Face is arguably one of Bangkok's coolest destinations with some of the most relaxing settings around. Home to a bar, Indian, Japanese

and Thai restaurants, with Lan Na Thai offering the best cuisine, the enclosed complex is modelled on a traditional Thai home that has been constructed from recovered teak timbers, with the earthenware roof tiles handmade by local artisans.

Authentic antiques from across Asia decorate the interiors of all of the buildings and you do pay a premium for the surrounds, but what surrounds they are.

Bangkok Face Sukhumvit 38
Tel: 02-713 6048 Website: www.facebars.com

Tempting Tacos

There's probably no easier way to transform your typical foodie into a pistol-toting bandolero than by starting an argument over the supposed authenticity of food served at any Mexican restaurant.

But if you've never been to Mexico and appreciate good food, then who really cares? From this perspective, La Monita Taqueria is probably the best Mexican-style restaurant in Bangkok. The unpretentious cantina with its bold orange walls and green tables and chairs is inspired by the streets of Vera Cruz, Los Angeles and San Francisco. Burritos, tacos, quesadillas, nachos, tortas and more are served in waxed paper-lined baskets. Weekly specials include barbacoa, ceviche and lengua. The chilli steak fries are mouth-watering and the heuvos rancheros is one of the best in town.

La Monita Taqueria 888/26 Mahatun Plaza, Sukhumvit Road
Tel: 02-650 9581 Website: www.lamonita.com
Closed Sundays

Hola, Hola

For years Bangkok lacked a decent Spanish restaurant, despite the myriad of cuisines available in the city. Tapas Café put paid to that shortfall when it opened on a little side street off Sukhumvit Soi 11.

High, black-framed windows and a mezzanine floor maximise the light in the small restaurant, which also doubles as a contemporary art gallery. Daily specials, which complement the extensive but not exhaustive menu of embutidos, tapas and paella, are chalked up on blackboards. These are supported by a reasonable wine list and a few special beers, including Ferran Adria's Inedit.

The place is abuzz with regulars on most evenings as Tapas has built its reputation on fast, attentive service and consistent quality. It may not be the best Spanish cuisine in Asia, but it is dependable and you can order safe in the knowledge that your meal will be good and hearty. *Albondigas con tomate*, *chipirones plancha* and *boquerones en vinagre* are especially good. There are also well-priced set menus during lunch.

They recently opened a new venue on Silom Soi 4 called Spanish on 4.

Tapas Cafe Sukhumvit Soi 11
Tel: 02-651 2947 Website: www.tapasiarestaurants.com

Surf, No Turf

Unsurprisingly, there's a distinct marine theme to The Seafood Bar's unpretentious open-plan design, with its drawcard being the massive oyster bar where Thailand's most extensive range of the mouthwatering molluscs are on display – there are 39 types of oysters on the menu with 15 or more typically in stock at any time.

Billy Marinelli, a marine biologist turned high-end international fishmonger, has been anointed the oyster king of Thailand since he opened The Oyster Bar (Narathiwas Soi 24, Tel: 02-219 4809, www.theoysterbarbangkok.com) a few years back. The Seafood Bar has followed hot on the heels of its predecessor's success, but with its larger space and a more elaborate kitchen the new venture can prepare a much wider range of seafood.

Range and quality are not the restaurant's only appeal; it's one of the few places in Southeast Asia that only serves fish and seafood in a western style. Plus, no turf (meat) will ever make its way onto the menu in this surf-only restaurant.

The Seafood Bar is closed Mondays and fish is delivered fresh on Tuesdays and Fridays. The all-you-can-eat Sunday lunch buffet, where you can order anything off the menu for 1,500 baht and get a free glass of sparkling wine, offers unparalleled value.

The Seafood Bar 41/2 Somerset Lake Point, Soi Sukhumvit 16
Tel: 02-663 8863 Website: www.theseafoodbar.info

THEOYSTERBAR

Crunch Munch

It's hard to think how one could indulge in a more virtuous meal than by munching your way through the crisp, organic vegetables and macrobiotic wonders at Sustaina.

Situated above an organic shop of the same name, Sustaina fulfils its simple and clear agenda of serving healthy food at affordable prices. There are vegan, vegetarian and macrobiotic options, as well as a reasonable choice of fish and chicken dishes, although there's no red meat served at the restaurant. The cuisine is mainly a combination of Japanese and Thai influences, but nothing is overly complicated and the quality of the ingredients is always at the forefront, with subtle dressings and sauces enhancing the natural flavours rather than smothering them.

Set meals range from about 250 to 500 baht and there's an extensive range of juices and herbal teas to choose from. Alcohol is also served.

Sustaina Sukhumvit Soi 39
Tel: 02-258 9766

Culinary Agent

Many restaurateurs have a story, apocryphal or otherwise, about the sequence of events that landed them in the food trade. Meyung Robson's tale, however, is likely to trump them all. The Vietnam native served as an FBI agent for two decades and she was tasked with working with the Vietnamese authorities at a time when relations between the country and Uncle Sam were frosty to say the least. In 2005, after collecting her pension and running for the door – "I gave them 20 years of my life and that was enough" – she opened Xuan Mai on Sukhumvit Soi 13. However, her business partner, the chef, bolted on opening night, leaving Meyung holding the baby and forcing her to take her hobby of cooking to another level.

Fortunately, she stepped up to the plate and then some. Xuan Mai has established itself as one of, if not the best Vietnamese restaurants in town. Now located on Thong Lor, the tastefully-converted shophouse doesn't try to compete with the area's chic dining destinations, but whatever it lacks in terms of design it makes up for with the wonderfully fresh cuisine on offer.

With some 80-odd dishes available, depending on season and what's at the market, there's plenty to choose from, but the best way to experience Xuan Mai is to ask Meyung for her recommendations. Do that and you're probably in for some off-menu specials such as the super-crunchy deep fried cassava.

Xuan Mai On the corner of Thong Lor/Thong Lor Soi 17
Tel: 02-185 2619 Website: www.xuanmairestaurant.com
Closed Mondays. Reservations essential on the weekend.

Soulful Dining

Food writer turned restaurateur Jarrett Wrisley founded Soul Food Mahanakorn (Mahanakorn means Bangkok in Thai) on a simple premise – wholesome ingredients, honest cooking and serious drinks. And it is the simplicity of this proposition that has made this unimposing Thai restaurant such a success.

Since arriving in Bangkok after spending seven years in China, mostly in Szechuan province, Jarrett has scoured the country for hidden recipes and regional specialities while writing about food for *The Atlantic* magazine.

Now, as a close acquaintance of the kingdom's culinary traditions, he has put the fruits of his labours into action. The menu at Soul Food comprises a broad range of dishes from across Thailand and its borders, and all are served with the chef's own personal touch (such as adding crunchy, deep-fried onions to the *gaeng hung lae*), but all of the recipes retain a fidelity with their traditional origins. A number of the dishes are seasonal, for example the *yum som o* (spicy pomelo salad) is only served when the fruit is plump and succulent, and the chalkboard also features a number of specials which are changed depending on what the market has to offer on any given day. Many of the ingredients are organic or sourced from smallholdings to ensure consistent quality.

The restaurant has two floors and is large enough for groups while maintaining an intimate atmosphere. The bar, which is situated in the main dining area on the ground floor, provides an alternative for those wanting to investigate the drinks list more than sample the food. The cocktails feature both classics and Soul Food specialities which make use of Thai ingredients such as Mekong rum, lemongrass and basil seeds. All drinks are double pours.

Soul Food Mahanakorn Soi Thong Lor
Tel: 02-714 7708 Website: www.soulfoodmahanakorn.com

Modern Mezze

Serenade has many things in common with the recent explosion of more creative restaurants aimed at diners who are not put off by experimenting and trying new dishes. It's located in a hip area – the green surrounds of Grass on Thong Lor – and the design is both minimalist and spacious, it has al fresco seating and is definitely a place where you can go to "be seen". What sets it apart from its contemporaries, however, is that rather than charging as much as possible, reasonable prices encourage diners to eat outside of the box – you can have a meal with a drink for about 800 baht a head.

The menu is broadly divided into four main areas: vegan and vegetarian, for your belly (starches), for the carnivores (meat) and stuff that swims (fish). Most of the dishes, which are served in relatively small mezze-sized portions, combine Thai and western influences. The results are normally a success with must tries including the "McNaem", a duck egg wrapped in house-made Naem sausage, fried and served on a Isaan chili cabbage slaw; risotto with fresh herbs and shitake mushroom; and seared American sea scallops on mashed garlic with mandarin reduction.

The menu is adapted and changed on a regular basis and there's always a few more interesting creations using molecular experimentalism and sous vide.

Serenade Grass, Thong Lor
Tel: 02-519 2365 Website: www.serenadebkk.com

It's All About Eggs

The neoclassical frontispiece of Omu contrasts with its glass walls and polished wood interiors, which while not constructed from pine, are more reminiscent of Scandinavia rather than Japan. But then omu rice itself is an odd, perhaps slightly confused invention from the Land of the Rising Sun and this two-floor eatery specialises in tasty fried rice wrapped in a Japanese omelette.

There is an unexpectedly broad range of fried rice fillings and sauces on offer, plus you can select the "volcano" (runny egg) option. Sets are available too and you can upsize your meal with a wafu burger to boot. If, however, you fancy something a little less cholesterol-laden, then sample the deserts on offer at the café next door.

Omu Japanese Omurice & Café Park Lane, Soi Ekamai
Tel: 02-382 0138

Delectable Deconstruction

There's a very traditional foundation to the design at Sra Bua by Kiin Kiin, the Kempinski Hotel's joint venture with Henrik Yde-Andersen, who runs the Michelin-starred Kiin Kiin in Copenhagen. Elongated polished teak pillars reach towards high ceilings, ornate salas are topped with elaborately carved roves and light sculptures are decorated with *chufa* designs. Chef Henrik's cuisine, however, couldn't be further away from "traditional" conceptions of how Thai food should be served. While using the best ingredients and traditional methods for making curry pastes and other essential components (everything is made fresh each day), he takes a radical, deconstructive approach to the way his food is served: textures, temperatures and presentation are played around with to create a culinary journey in each dish.

For example, liquid nitrogen is used to create a red curry terrine, as opposed to the traditional soup base, yet the flavours remain perfectly balanced and well within the traditional context.

The Harvest, one of the signature dishes, is composed of a green curry mouse served in a earthenware flower pot with cookie crumbs sprinkled on top to represent soil, and an organic carrot protruding through the surface. Not what you expect to be served in a Thai restaurant, but an experience that is unforgettable.

Chef Henrik flies in every three months to create a new menu and train the staff, who provide attentive service, introduce each course and explain how to eat it.

Sra Bua has no a la carte options, there's a five-course lunch menu for 1,500 baht which takes about an hour to finish. The 7- and 11-course dinners take up to two-and-a-half hours. Wine or homemade fruit juice paring options are also available.

Sra Bua by Kiin Kiin Siam Kempinski Hotel Bangkok, 991/9 Rama 1 Road
Tel 02-162 9000 Website: www.kempinski.com

East Meets East

About 20 years ago, some Israelis who were passing through Bangkok taught a couple of eager Thais how to cook home-style schnitzel, hummus and hazilim. Since then, Shoshana has been a huge hit with locals and tourists alike.

The small restaurant is a friendly, family-run affair and while the prices have increased significantly over the past few years, they are still ridiculously cheap. Chicken schnitzel with hummus, hazilim and potato salad costs 180 baht. There's a range of dips, including labane, tahina and tzatziki, fresh pitas and other regional standards such as falafel, a wonderfully piquant Moroccan carrot salad and shakshuka. The fried chicken liver is also excellent.

Shoshana 86 Chakrapong Road
Tel: 02-282 9948

Vegetarian Delights

The staff at Anotai clearly take the ideology of the slow food movement to heart. At times it feels as if glaciers could collide before they take your order, but the wait is always worth it and given the fact that this vegetarian restaurant is in a slightly hard to get to location, you'll probably want to relish your dining time anyway.

The menu mainly comprises Japanese and Thai dishes, with a few pasta and soup options. Some of the starters are exceptional, such as the seaweed wrapped tofu with wasabi mayonnaise. Every dish, be it *laab tofu* or a spicy cucumber salad, has its own distinctive treatment and Anotai is best enjoyed in a group of three or more so you sample a wider range of dishes. There's a tempting selection of wholesome – but certainly not calorie-free – desserts such as chocolate cake, brownies and scones flavoured with blueberry, lemon zest and prunes.

Anotai Soi Rama 9 Hospital
Tel: 02-641 5366

Curry Fried Future

If you want molecular gastronomy talk to a scientist, but if you're game for a radical approach to Indian cuisine, Gaggan Anand is your man.

As the first Indian and second Asian to study under Michelin-starred Spanish chef Ferran Adria, Gaggan is certainly unique in the progressive approach he has taken to his homeland's diverse cuisine.

Techniques such as "spherication", using gelling agents to make sphere-like foods, is applied to spiced yoghurts and reconstructed lentils, ensuring all the flavour is delivered instantly. His kitchen, which every diner is taken on a tour of, features traditional Indian utensils such as a tandoor and massive copper vessels, as well as equipment that is more typically seen in a scientific laboratory; including condensers for extracting flavours from anything from coffee to foie gras, liquid nitrogen on tap and temperature-controlled water baths.

The Calcutta native's menu includes more traditional dishes, such as mutton bhuna ghosh, which is slow cooked sous vide-style, and mussels topped with a curry foam, and more abstract creations such as his Three Acts of Foie Gras which serves the liver glazed, as a powder and as a terrine.

The 10-course tasting menu is the best way to enjoy your first visit to Gaggan. Be sure to book the Chef's Table, which affords a view of the

Gaggan Langsuan (opposite Langsuan Soi 3)
Tel: 02-652 1700 Website: www.eatatgaggan.com

kitchen at work. While the experience is amazing and the location in a
restored wooden house adds to the atmosphere, what stands out the most
is Gaggan's passion and enthusiasm for his craft.

Tasting Trends

This recent arrival on Bangkok's dining scene combines a hip music bar with a prime dining venue. Salt's sleek concrete and glass bar and restaurant contrasts with the al fresco seating, an outside pizza bar and extra space in the renovated wooden house at the back of the compound.

It's as much a place to hang out and drink with friends as it is a dining destination and you can choose to stretch out on comfy cushions on the grass lawn or sit at the outside bar next to the wood-fired pizza oven and watch laser projections on the building's exterior.

If you do choose to eat, there's a dependable range of Japanese, Italian and international fare. Reservations are advised given its appeal with the affluent local Thai and expat community.

Salt Soi Aree
Tel: 02-619 6886
Closed Mondays

Fire in the Blood

Somtumized's relaxed atmosphere incorporates rustic elements, little pots used in witchcraft and a wiry tree decorated with polaroids of previous customers. The seating is simple, with wooden benches covered in Thai sarongs fitted snugly against the long timber benches.

On the surface at least, the restaurant appears to be just another trendy outlet serving fiery Isaan cuisine from Thailand's northeast. Closer examination of the menu, however, reveals a greater level of thought than one may at first assume. The name "Somtumized" comes from "*som tum*", the spicy papaya salad, and "customised", as chef Kingkan Salakonthanavat has put together menu with different variations of *som tum* tailored for different blood types. According to Kingkan, *som tum* with pineapple and shrimps is best suited to people with type-O blood because they shouldn't eat too many peanuts and it contains plenty of iodine and calcium. Type-As, however, should feast on the pomelo *som tum* because it's high in vitamin C.

Fortunately, enjoying the food doesn't depend on whether or not you subscribe to this holistic belief. The chef's additional scrutiny has resulted in fresh, tasty dishes which avoid the pervasive Thai trend to over-sweeten everything. The *gaeng saeb*, a curry which is served in a copper chafing dish, is superbly spicy and sour, while the *khor moo yang* (grilled pork neck) is wonderfully succulent. Prices range from 69 to 300 baht, with most dishes at the cheaper end of the scale.

Somtumized Mansion 7, Ratchadapisek Soi 14
Tel: 02-275 1489

CAFÉ CULTURE

Peace **and Prosperity**

While Bangkok boasts a plethora of cafes, the city is home to few teahouses, which is why Hundred Children is worth a mention. The two-floor venue is furnished with original and restored antiques imported from China; in fact you can buy pretty much everything you can see in the shop. Arnake Reungkitjanuwa transformed one of his family's old antiques shops into the teahouse in a bid to give their business a shot in the arm. All things considered, the move was a success and the place now serves as a popular meeting place. A range of Chinese teas and Hundred Children's own brand coffee is served alongside a range of home-baked cookies and cakes.

Hundred Children Café & Gallery Corner of Sukhumvit Soi 14
Tel: 081-813 3523 Website: hundredchildren.blogspot.com

Made in Manhattan

While a number of boutique bakeries have sprung up around Bangkok over the past few years, there has, until recently, remained a dearth of proper fresh, chewy, US-style bagels.

Fortunately, Eric Seldin, a TV cameraman who has resided in Bangkok for 20 years, decided it was time for change and in March 2011 he opened the doors to the Bangkok Bagel Factory. Through the smart use of Twitter and Facebook, he has managed to quickly build a reputation for what is seen by many as the only authentic New York deli in town.

Everything is made on the premises by the chef, who like Eric also hails from Manhattan, using Thai ingredients. There are no processed meats or cheeses to be seen and Norwegian salmon and American turkey are the only imported items on the menu.

Yummy home-baked cookies, brownies and other sweet treats are also on offer and make the perfect accompaniment to a cup of hot Thai robusta.

Bangkok Bagel Bakery GF Maneeya Center, Ploenchit Road
Tel: 02-254 8157 Website: www.bkkbagelbakery.com
Closed Sundays

Bread Head

French cuisine has had something of a renaissance in Thailand over the past couple of years, but the results were a mixed success with too many restaurants trying too hard with little success.

While it positions itself as little more than a traditional Parisian café-boulangerie, Café Tartine is probably the most authentic French eatery in Bangkok. The fact that it is always full of French expats pays testament to the quality of its offering. Not only does it bake the finest French batons in town, complete with the trademark crunchy, chewy crust and light centre, it's also one of the only places where you can enjoy a bowl of hot chocolate or coffee in which to dunk your croissant or *pain au chocolat*.

While it's open everyday from 8am to 8pm, the best time to come is for brunch or lunch, although you would be advised to make a booking. Beyond the excellent croc monsieur, sandwiches and the hearty make-your-own salads is a range of soups and a selection of cheeses and meats from the charcuterie. Be warned though, the portions are deceptively generous.

Café Tartine The Athenee Residence, Soi Ruamrudee
Tel: 02-168 5464 Website: www.cafetartine.net

BAGUETTE   SALADE   CROISSANT

All's Well
That Eats Well

Nature-inspired décor featuring cut-out green and white leaves festoon the walls and ceiling at THANN Cafe, where organic woven rattan lamps offer subdued lighting, and tables and chairs are fashioned from biodegradable products.

The bistro is a spinoff from one of the country's best-known producers of aromatic spa and beauty products, a selection of which can be purchased here. However, given the THANN mothership's focus on wellness, one might expect the cuisine on offer here to be a little more health obsessed – beside dishes such as Green Pea Soup with Ginkgo or Khao Soi Duck Confit, the deserts such as tiramisu and layer cake are far more decadent than what most spa cafes would serve.

THANN Café Fl1 Gaysorn Plaza, Ploenchit Road
Tel: 02-656 1060 Website: www.thann.info

Mellow Vibes

Despite its location and the fact that it has been open for years, Bitter Brown remains one of Bangkok's best-kept secrets with most old hands unaware of its presence. The husband and wife team behind the place say they are "low key" and never bother to do much marketing, relying mainly on word of mouth for their trade.

Their laid-back approach has helped form the café's relaxed environment, where colourful abstract paintings from Thai artists hang on the walls and you can choose to sit at a dining table, on plush sofas or grab the super comfy opium bed if you get there early enough. The coffee is great, as is the international food such as spaghetti with spicy anchovy sauce or grilled mushroom salad.

There's also free Wi-Fi (but bring a charged battery as there are no power outlets) and a decent selection of magazines, coffee table books and the odd mass market thriller to choose from.

Bitter Brown Asoke Court, Soi Asoke (about 200 metres along from the entrance to Soi Cowboy)
Tel: 02-261 6535
Closed Saturday and Sunday

Electric Kool-Aid Jewellery Test

One has to wonder if the Bapitchayanggul sisters Khempisa and Kunyachat slipped something into their Kool-Aid when they were dreaming up the décor for Montra Jewelry Café. There's a hallucinogenic quality to the place which sports velveteen stools, tiny babyfoot tables, hanging womb chairs and a faux bookshelf on the main wall.

If the mammoth clown doesn't weird you out, things get stranger still on weekends as a the cafe's stock of ukuleles and small guitars attracts an odd crowd of people who are happy to sit either in groups or by themselves and spend their time strumming away.

The sisters' jewellery is displayed in shelves and cases tucked away in the corners, with a range of sterling silver and big bead costume designs on offer.

Montra Café & Gallery GF Yada Building, Silom Road
Tel: 02-652 4462 Website: www.montrajewelry.com

Home from Home

The kids behind Sugar Lust Café & Bistro have taken a "cozy like home" approach to this neat little hangout located in a 40-year old house. Soft seating and beanbags, both inside and on the lawn, make it conducive to sitting around and chilling with friends. And there's a range of Thai and fusion cuisine on offer, plus a host of treats from the Sugar Lust home bakery, including Banoffee Pie, Double Chocolate Cheesecake and Apple Crumble Cheesecake with Maple Syrup Sauce.

Sugar Lust also stays open late, until midnight on Tuesdays to Thursdays and 1.30am for the rest of the week, so on top of the expected teas and coffee is a decent range of beers, wine and cocktails to make the longer nights more conversational.

Sugar Lust Cafe & Bistro Sukhumvit Soi 26
Tel: 084-011 4115 Website: www.sugarlustcafe.com

Soi 38

Sukhumvit Soi 38 reigns as *the* destination for street food in Bangkok, with a massive range of some of the best seafood, curries, noodles and chicken. While the range has waned in recent years the quality of food is great and if you're a bit nervous about trying stuff from the street then this is a good place to break your cherry. Be sure to sample the *khao man gai* (steamed or fried chicken on rice) or *khao moo daeng* (red pork on rice), either of which is best followed up with *khao niaow mamuang*, sticky rice soaked in coconut milk and topped with luscious ripe mango.

Soi Arab

For the best selection of Middle Eastern food head to Sukhumvit Soi 3/1, otherwise known as Soi Arab. This narrow lane is home to a host of shops and restaurants catering to the local Arab community. It only takes a few steps down the soi to enter this micro-community which has a completely different atmosphere to the rest of the city's side streets: the whole place has a much more shiny feel to it thanks to the plethora of mirrors, coloured glass and polished metal that decorate the streetside restaurants; the smell of kebabs and scented tobacco from sheesha pipes mingle in the air, and Arabic languages become the area's *lingua franca*.

Unsurprisingly, it's an alcohol-free area and most of the cuisine is Egyptian with a few Lebanese and other regional restaurants thrown in.

Chinatown

Everything seems bigger and better in Chinatown, from the piles of oversized animal innards and pomelos to the fresh fish and seafood on offer.

Wander down Yaowarat Road at any time of day and you can get something freshly cooked to eat, from steamed dumplings to *kuay tiaow phed* (duck noodles). But the best experience to be had is after dark. The neon glare from the trademark Chinese signs light up the streets and the pavement fills with small stalls selling an unparalleled range of food. TK Seafood on the corner of Phadung Dao and Yoawarat roads has been serving barbequed, steamed and curried fish and seafood for years – the crab fried with black pepper or curry sauce is especially good – but there are several similar street stalls that are worth checking out which are open from late afternoon to past midnight. If they're busy with locals, they're generally good.

If you still have room for pudding, stop off at one of the smaller stalls selling hot Chinese deserts cooked in largish copper vessels and ask for *bua loy naam king*, black sesame dumplings in ginger tea.

shopping

ANCY PICKING UP A MASERATI OR AMBORGHINI, OR MAYBE SOMETHING MORE DOWN T HEEL SUCH AS A YAMAGUCHI HIFI OR A SWAROVSKI RING? 'HATEVER YOU'RE AFTER, YOU CAN BE PRETTY SURE THAT IT AN BE FOUND IN ONE OF THE CITY'S MULTITUDE OF MALLS, ARKETS AND SHOPPING DISTRICTS.

BANGKOK IS A SHOPPER'S PARADISE. WITHIN A FEW OURS YOU CAN HAGGLE FOR GOODS AT A LOCAL MARKET, HECK OUT THE LATEST FASHIONS BY LOCAL DESIGNERS AND ROWSE THE WINDOWS OF THE CITY'S MOST EXPENSIVE OUTIQUES.

THE NOUGHTIES WITNESSED THE RISE OF THE LUXURY HOPPING CENTRE (MANY OF WHICH IN REALITY ARE LITTLE ORE THAN HIGH-END RETAIL MUSEUMS), WHILE THE LAST EW YEARS HAVE SEEN THE EMERGENCE OF SO-CALLED OMMUNITY MALLS; LOW-RISE CENTRES WHICH ACT AS UTLETS FOR SMALL, STANDALONE BRANDS THAT EXHIBIT A AGGERING DIVERSITY OF DESIGNS.

THERE'S NO DOUBT THAT FLAIR AND CREATIVITY RE IN ABUNDANCE IN THIS TOWN. READ ON TO CHECK OUT OME OF THE BEST PURVEYORS OF DIMESTORE CHIC, RETRO HREADS AND CONTEMPORARY URBAN FASHION.

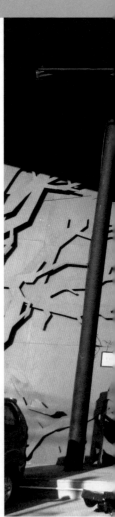

Spooked Out

Mansion 7 is without a doubt Bangkok's coolest shopping centre, after all what other city can boast its own "boutique thriller mall"? The entrance, over which a 10-metre ghoul-like hand towers, leads into a darkened covered warehouse populated with creepy fairground attractions. Small standalone structures house shops selling anything from clothes and shoes to magic gimmicks and bondage gear, while bars, restaurants and a clairvoyant's stall are built into the perimeter. The facade of the haunted house occupies the entire rear wall.

The development is big on creativity, and while certainly quirky, Mansion 7 will hopefully avoid aging too quickly and ending up as the kitsch hangover of some developer's overactive imagination. It has also been intelligently designed and constructed in a way that makes the location affordable for smaller, local brands which adds to its allure and helps it stand out from the plethora of more sanitised malls in Bangkok.

Mansion 7 Ratchadapisek Soi 14
Tel: 02-692 631 Website: www.themansion7.com
Open Mon-Fri noon-midnight, Sat-Sun noon-2am

Step to it

As the name suggests, this family business started from humble origins in 1959 by knocking out ballet shoes for the local market at a time when wannabe Anna Pavlovas found it tough to get the right footwear. Since then, Ballet Shoes (which has other branches at Siam Square and id1) has transformed itself into a contemporary brand catering to fashion conscious women. There's still a neat simplicity to the designs, which predominantly feature bold monochrome colours, but there's plenty of diversity in terms of shape and materials used. Prices range from about 900 to 3,000 baht a pair, and the designs can be customised and made-to-measure for an additional 300 baht.

Ballet Shoes
Tel: 02-275 1317 Website: www.balletsince1959.com

Armed and
Dangerous

Cris Horwang has become a household name in Thailand for both her looks and attitude. The former ballet dancer turned model, actress, radio DJ and designer breaks the mould by refusing to play the role of the cutesy airhead. She simply doesn't do stereotypes and this is evident in the designs at Secret Weapon Lab. Big, bold oversized bags fashioned from sheepskin and leather in colours ranging from classic browns to bright orange, yellows and deep ocean blue are priced from 3,000 to 9,500 baht. Form and function meet practical elements such as detachable nylon inners and multiple phone holders. There's an arsenal of accessories and sunglasses on offer too.

Secret Weapon Lab
Tel: 02-276 0155 Website: secretweaponlab.com

SIAM SQUARE

Where's My Handbag

In 1998, a group of Thai friends decided to rebel against the banal array of shoddy quality bags and ridiculously overpriced clutches by producing a range of bags that you'd happy to be seen with. Good Old Days focuses on quality workmanship and a subtle simplicity underpins all of the designs (which are handmade from either imported canvas or leather), from the classic appeal of the briefcases and portmanteaux to the vibrant orange Ball and Mag designs.

There's a bag for every occasion, for both men and women (priced 2,000 to 10,600 baht), plus a range of hippie-fied dresses from Hong Kong, Vietnam, Indonesia and Japan ranging from 500 to 3,000 baht.

Good Old Days Siamkit Building, GF, Siam Square Soi 7
Tel: 02-250 7363 Website: www.goodolddaysshop.com

Fill Me Up

Thailand is full of great designers and clothing brands, but too often many of them are designed for Thai-sized people – think svelte, skinny and well proportioned and you get the general picture. So if you can work your way into a pair of drainpipe jeans without the aid of a crowbar, you may want to pick up a pair of Thanarad Mayteedol's denims. Being a unisex brand, there's an androgynous mode to Gasoline & Garage. While the black and bleach wash designs appear mainly for indie kids and emo rockers, there are also brighter colours, such as pinks and indigos for people who know how to smile too. Jeans go for 1,600 to 1,850 baht, with the more extravagant designs fetching up to 2,600 baht. Shorts cost 1,290 baht and shirts start from 750 baht.

Gasoline & Garage F1 Siamkitti Building, Siam Square
Tel: 081-456 4272
Open daily from 11am to 9pm

Secret Garden

With its iron door, wrought iron grills and tunnel-like interior, Rotsaniyom evokes a sense of place akin to a scene from The Secret Garden or a Handmade Films period production. If this was Off Phongsak and Gift Thida's intention then it provides the perfect backdrop to their vintage designs – which they describe as "natural ethnic" and "old bohemian" – that pay homage to the 1920s with wide-brimmed floppy cotton hats, simple knee-length dresses and crocheted shawls. Prices range from 490 to 2,500 baht.

Rotsaniyom Siam Square Soi 5
Tel: 081-304 2198 Website: www.rotsaniyom.com

Wardrobe of Wonders

Surita Urapongsa's studies in New York left a permanent impression upon her, something that would eventually manifest in a unique, if not slightly schizophrenic expression when she returned to Thailand.

It's Happened to be a Closet is, well, quite closet-like, with an exterior akin to a New York/Irish bar, complete with gold-tinted windows and dark stained wood. As for the interior, imagine *Dr Who's* Tardis crossed with the closet from *The Lion, The Witch and the Wardrobe* and you'll get halfway there, sort of. Venture inside and you'll find stacks of new clothes in piles, displayed on shelves and other places. Grab a seat and have a coffee downstairs or head upstairs to the open kitchen and restaurant at the back. Clothes start at about 2,000 baht up to 100,000 baht for a full-blown ballgown.

While there are other branches at Siam Paragon and Emporium, the Siam Square branch is simply the best. It's a great place to relax and have a drink in air-conditioned climes before embarking on a good old rummage. For a different perspective from the same designer take a trip through the looking glass to Palette, across the road at Siam Center, where the designs are much more trendy and contemporary.

It's Happened to be a Closet Siam Square Soi 3
Tel: 02-658 4696 Website: itshappenedtobeacloset.wordpress.com

Mellowed Out Punk

It's hard to work out where exactly I Love NoName is coming from with its designs: dresses range from subdued floral prints and more conservative designs (which could almost be classified as workwear save for the suspender collar accessories), to punked-out textile assemblages and tribal ethnic miniskirts. But then, not knowing what to expect is not such a bad thing, and the Chansawas sisters' dynamism is likely to keep the fashion hounds coming through the door.

Most of the clothes range from 380 to 1,600 baht, although the boots, which include customised fluorescent pink 16-hole Doc Martens, sell at around the 10,000 baht mark.

I Love NoName Siam Square Soi 5
Tel: 086-534 6335 Website: ilovenoname.com

Hangout **Homes**

Eight years of study in the US sparked Bob Varakrit's passion for footwear, culminating in his opening of VII Athletic Club, a boutique which boasts one of Bangkok's best ranges of trainers from major brands such as Nike and Adidas, to lesser known makes like DC, Royal Elastic and Fubu.

Despite the fanaticism that often surrounds the subculture of street footwear, V.A.C. has an attitude-free environment – the staff is both knowledgeable and friendly and will happily help or leave you to browse the three floors as you wish. In fact, part of Bob's vision for the shop is to help educate Thais about trainers and create a space where they can come and hang out as much as shop.

Beyond the footwear, V.A.C. sells women's wear, vintage clothing, basketball and football products, as well as its own line of silverwear, accessories, bling rings and watches under the Victim of Vanity label. Shoes cost between 2,000 to 7,500 baht, clothes are mostly priced from 700 to 1890 baht, with Victim of Vanity products fetching 1,200 to 5,000 baht.

VII Athletic Club Siam Square Soi 1
Tel: 084-705 7744 Website: www.viiathleticclub.com

Green Mind

The lamentable range of environment-friendly products available in Thailand spurred Thai TV host and actor Pipat "Top" Apiraktanakorn to open Eco Shop to showcase goods that combine cutting-edge design with a green outlook.

Top now has his own line of eco-friendly products – he studied design prior to entering the media world – and personally selects everything on display at this open-plan store. His concept of sustainability extends beyond the array of locally and internationally-made low energy lamps, wooden mouse mats and bags made from recycled rubber tyres; social development is also a key part of the paradigm shift he thinks is needed to created a more equitable future for the planet. As such, Eco Shop employs a number of deaf people as staff, so be patient if they don't immediately understand what you say.

Eco Shop Digital Gateway, Siam Square
Tel: 087-099 0639 Website: www.ecoshop.in.th

Minimalist Masters

The minimalism of Kan'ser menswear is guided by the local fashion label's mantra – "Less but better". There's an unusual combination of modish and garage punk influences in the range of men's shorts, tees and shirts, especially with the long sleeve tees which echo the classic Buzzcocks tops. Most designs feature two-tone colours, typically black, whites and greys, with subtle pinks and blues being about as vivid as it gets.

Contrast and custom cuts are the other dominant features, be it the colours themselves or the use of other materials and patterns, such as tartan panels stitched onto the back of shirts.

Prices are very reasonable with shorts at 490 baht, shirts from 790 baht, and trousers and tees at 790 baht and 390 baht respectively.

Kan'ser Lido, Siam Square
Website: www.kansershop.com

Alternative Threads

Since 1999, WWA has been providing an alternative to mainstream clothing for men and women, created by a trio of designers who are driven by a desire to create usable fashion that transcends normal boundaries and concepts.

There's great diversity on offer and while some of the creations are suitable for everyday wear, some of the more radical, deconstructed designs, which incorporate fake ostrich feathers and satin, will require a more adventurous disposition to step out in.

Price ranges from 1,500 to 20,000 baht.

WWA 3rd floor, Siam Square Soi 7
Tel: 02-658 4686 Website: www.wwa.co.th

Passionate Pioneer

Ad industry legend Bhanu Inkawat has played a fundamental role in developing the Thai fashion industry ever since he opened the doors of his first Greyhound store in 1980. For a decade, his team focused on producing classy menswear aimed at creative workers and artists who thrived on the energy of the post-punk generation, before branching out into women's wear and launching Playhound urban clothing.

Greyhound is all about simplicity and there's and abundance of black, white, greys and light blues tones in the almost sombre designs. While the label now has several shops around the city and a number of bistro cafes, it still remains true to its innovative origins and continues to inspire new generations of Thai designers.

Greyhound/Playhound 3rd floor Siam Center
Tel: 02-251 4917 Website: www.greyhound.co.th

Mountain Men

Drawing inspiration from a Tibetan song of the same name, 10,000 Miles Through the Himalayas is Wattanakiat Phatcharachokmongkol's outlet for his Q and T-Play clothing and Qubisch footwear brands. He says the latest collection is inspired by the need to escape the urban condition and draws inspiration from the Silk Road, Asia Minor and Mediterranean blending of cool colours and warm tones. Expect to find black or white drainpipe jeans, striped tops and white hoodies.

T-Play tees take a different approach, incorporating geometric shapes, Rorschach-style patterns and more surreal animal imagery. Qubisch offers a range of simple light-toned shoes and handmade desert boots.

10,000 Miles Through the Himalayas Mob F, Siam Center
Tel: 081-299 5871 Website: www.qillstyle.com

10,000 Miles Through
The Himalayas
spring/summer 2011

Easy Wearing

There's something grand about Siriorn Teankaprasith's vision for
PAINKILLER, which she explains as "a medicine that reduces pain, the
alternative menswear". Neither too feminine or masculine, or metrosexual
for that fact, the clothing suitably balances form and function.

There's a full range of semi-formal/casual wear for men, including
shoes and accessories, with a classic 1930s European influence. Some
designs are more dramatic, such as the zoot suits which make an
unashamed use of light colours, beiges, mustards and oranges. But
whatever Siriorn lays her hand to, she always remains dedicated to detail,
with fine needlework and intricate patterns becoming more apparent on
closer inspection.

PAINKILLER Siam Center
Website: www.painkiller.wordpress.com

Threads **for** Thought

Twenty-something students and first-time workers are the target for PHIL Apparel's short-run lines of clothing for men. The limited edition approach ensures that the selection is always changing with the times. While most of the range of shirts, shorts, denim and trousers are simple and straightforward, there's a touch of the New Romantics added to many of the jackets and bolder designs. A fun-loving attitude binds the PHIL team who claim the idea for the label was born from a few spirited drinking sessions. PHIL is short for philosophical, and while it's hard to see exactly how the aesthetic has been inspired in part by Gandhian thinking, as they claim, they certainly seem to enjoy their work.

PHIL Siam Paragon FL2
Website: www.philapparel.com

Simply Special

NOXX is all about excelling at something very simple. Elegant T-shirts and tops, v-necks, tank tops and polo shorts made from 100% Pima cotton with minimal design and no labels or graphics showing. The colour range is limited, mostly black or white or greys, with additional pink options for women. At the end of the day it's all about the touch and feel of the clothes and designer Wasu "Nox" Manomaiphibul, says the extra "x" in "Noxx" emphasises the extra softness. All products cost 690 or 890 baht.

NOXX Fl 2, Paragon Department Store (Menswear Section)
Tel: 081-812 2340 Website: www.facebook.com/noxxshop

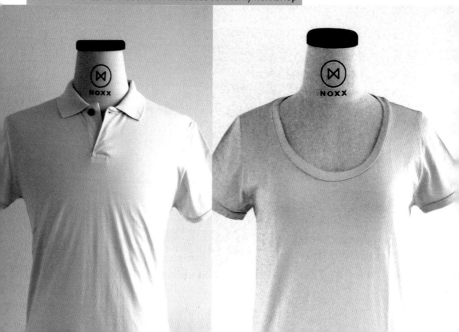

RATCHAPRASONG

Wanvisa & Mom **102** Golf R-Porn **103**
The Old Story **104** OAK **105** mantis **106**
Art of Comfort **107** Old School Chic **108** JBB* **110**

Fresh **Identity: id1**

There are few retail spaces that small, local designers can afford in the
Siam and Ratchaprasong area, which is home to most of Bangkok's luxury
shopping malls and high-end boutiques. id1, at the back of the ground
floor at Amarin Plaza, aims to counter this and the mostly open-plan space
is home to a number of permanent shops and stalls that are brimming
with originality and creativity.

Wanvisa & Mom

An industrious mother-and-daughter team produce the Wanvisa & Mom line of women's shoes and spike heels fashioned from cowhide and crocodile- and fish-skin, which cost 1,500 to 4,500 baht a pair. Most of the colours are loud and proud with a few more subtle tones to choose from, and there's a range of handbags that follow the same aesthetic theme. Bespoke services are also available.

Wanvisa & Mom
Tel: 086-335 2468

Golf **R-Porn**

For quirky women's accessories and chunky custom jewellery drop by Golf R-Porn, where the eponymous Mr Golf applies a slightly hallucinogenic sense of humour to his creations. You can find small earrings with prints of a young Audrey Hepburn, more bejewelled designs featuring acrylic crystals and a collection of sofa buttons, and loop chain necklaces with brightly coloured beads.

Golf R-Porn
Tel: 081-566 8815

The **Old** Story

The Old Story offers classic designs that draw on 1950s fashion with a smidgen of pre-war headwear and a hat's tip to the bold horizontal stripes of French onion sellers. The yesteryear aesthetic continues throughout the shop's interior and displays.

The Old Story
Tel: 081-372 6724

OAK

There's a distinctive difference between OAK's evening and casual wear, but both lines are notable for their contemporary, comfortable, no-nonsense designs.

Eveningwear ranges from light cotton dresses to figure-hugging cocktail numbers and longer, asymmetric dresses. There's an abundance of pastels and subtle monotone greys and beiges as well as some more vibrant floral patterns, which while colourful, are never garish. The casual wear makes use of block prints, cartoon characters and patterns in sequins or studs. Crop tops and tank tops use minimalist designs that are often adorned with ruffs. OAK also produces its own accessories, including handbags, purses and costume jewellery. Prices range from 300 to 2,500 baht.

OAK
Tel: 02-973 1179 Website: www.oakbkk.com

mantis

Mantis is worth a browse if you're into the understated simplicity of jeans and tees. Stocking mainly urbanwear for men, Mantis T-shirts and boxers are all about laidback comfort. Twenty August long-sleeve T-shirts printed with stencil-cut graffiti designs are also available for a few hundred baht.

Art of Comfort

Women with an itinerant nature may well find an ideal travelling companion at Nomad, where Toom and Jum's designs are all about carefree comfort. The duo was driven to action by the lack of casual, hippie clothing for women, especially those above 30 and 40 who are looking for "something casual in this youth focused market," says Jum.

Long, lofty dresses sporting impressionist floral patterns and patchwork designs, crochet brassieres and natural linen pinstripe trousers are handmade from high-quality textiles and are ideally suited to the fierce heat and humidity of the tropics. There's also a range of elegant gowns and dresses – while these adopt more formal lines and cuts, it doesn't stop the irreverent Nomad hippy chick from shining through.

Nomad
Tel: 081-720 6989

Old School Chic

Retro chic continues to gain ground in Bangkok, but what emerged in New York thrift stores and charity shops and second-hand clothes stalls in England has now been transformed into an increasingly sophisticated and pricy "vintage" market.

A few places in Bangkok now cater specifically for this market. After collecting vintage clothes for years, Joe opened SERENDIPITY to compliment his own Dress Garden designs and as an outlet to start selling from his collection of more than 1,000 dresses and other items sourced mainly from England and Japan. Prices are pretty reasonable and most range from 350 to 3,500 baht. Joe personally selects everything on sale in the store, noting that "while there are plenty of classic brands, I tend to go for style, being much more drawn by the look of an item of clothing than who made it". He says the serendipity comes from customers browsing until they find something they like, but it better fit as alterations are a big no-no.

Serendipity
Tel: 081-720 6989

Serendipity

JBB✳

Located next door to id1, the Grand Hyatt Erawan is home to Jirawat Bote Benchakarn's JBB✳ outlet. Bote seeks to redefine classic staples of a gentleman's wardrobe, such the navy blazer, tweed jacket, button-down shirt and chinos. In most cases his tweaking of these traditional designs are subtle and understated, but occasionally they incorporate unexpectedly loud colours, especially in the range of shorts, but JBB✳

is generally all about creating perfect shapes and proportions without unnecessary details.

Bote says he is targeting men who have tried out pretty much every genre and followed every trend in fashion but are still left wanting. His simple modern designs are aimed at people who crave details and appreciate good cloth and cuts, but who mostly want to look laidback rather than trying to make a loud statement.

The collection ranges from 1,200 baht for a bow tie up to 14,500 baht for a tailored jacket.

JBB Shop 01, Grand Hyatt Erawan, Rajadamri Road
Tel: 02-252 8786

Karmakamet

You'll probably become aware of Karmakamet before you see it as the scents from this aromatic apothecary give advance warning of its presence.

The dark wood shop, which is open on all sides, comprises a herbal tearoom and different sections where you can purchase fragrant products such as incense, handmade candles, soaps and body lotions and sprays (prices range from 165 to 2,350 baht). There's a full range of aromatherapy oils and massage products as well as its own brand of herbal teas, all of which are wrapped in vintage-style packaging.

While the brand has its humble origins in a stall at Chatuchak Market, it has become so successful that it now boasts its own hotel, The Scent, on Koh Samui.

Karmakamet CentralWorld, 2nd Fl, Zone C
Tel: 02-613 1397 Website: www.karmakamet.co.th

Tom Boy **Textiles**

Munchumart Numbenjapol, a former Playhound designer, has carved a name for herself over the past few years with her clothing which often feminises traditional masculine apparel. The designs also feature gowns and shorts suits that draw on elements from the 1930s and 1950s, as well as halter tops, miniskirts and futuristic silver leggings. Her playful designs incorporate a wide range of textiles that include silk, satin and chiffon. Each of Munchumart's collections is limited edition; she returns to the drawing board to dream up new designs once a particular range has sold out.

Munchu's CentralWorld, Floor 2, Rama 1 Road
Tel: 02-351 8018 Website: www.munchu-s.com

Child's Play

There's a child-like quality to the designs at Kloset, which founder Mollika Ruangkritya says stems from her fascination with making dolls and other toys when she was a little girl.

Over the past decade Kloset has expanded from simple casual wear into more elaborate couture and now also produces its own jewellery and accessories, but the focus on quality craftsmanship and handmade elements, such as stitching and embroidery, remains a signature of the brand.

Kloset Red Carpet was fairly recently launched to create a mature line of more sophisticated designs which still maintain fidelity to Mollika's original brand vision.

Kloset CentralWorld, Floor 2, Atrium zone
Tel: 02-646 1929 Website: www.klosetdesign.com

JATUJAK WEEKEND MARKET

Drift baby, drift

Jatujak (or Chatuchak) Weekend Market is the Thailand's largest market and one of the largest weekend markets in the world. It's absolutely massive, with more than 10,000 stalls in 28 sections drawing an estimated 200,000 visitors each Saturday and Sunday. Unsurprisingly, shopping at "JJ", as it's also known, can be a mental experience. It's hot, crowded and quite often disorienting, but great deals are to be found in this treasure trove of creativity where stalls range from boutique fashion brands to product design, home goods and contemporary art. What you get out of a visit to the market ultimately depends on the amount of time, effort and shoe leather you are prepared to expend, but the best way to experience the place is to drift with the crowd. An array of food stalls, bars and massage shops make excellent pit stops and if you can't handle the heat, head to the air-conditioned climes of the nearby JJ Mall.

For advanced planning check out www.jatujak-market.com

Jatujak Market Khampaeng Phed Road

Momoest

Suphachai Ketkaroonkul opened Momoest in mid-2010 as a venue from which to display and sell his more creative and less commercial works. Combining skills from his day job as a portrait photographer with more technical artistry (he studied art at Thammasat University and film in Paris, France) and mixed media to produce a range of diverse black and white and colour prints, which are defined either by organic natural forms or urban themes. Most pieces range from about 10,000 to 16,000 baht, which is pretty reasonable considering each one takes the artist about a week to produce.

Momoest Section 7, Soi 8
Tel: 089-680 8726 Website: www.momoest.co.th

Ego **Clay**

Fans of ceramics and bronze sculptures should check out Ego Clay, which also sells wall-sized abstract paintings for about 40,000 baht. Most of the sculptures draw on Asian and Buddhist themes, with the ceramics typically using a Raku-style cracked glaze, but the contemporary treatment they are given differentiates them from the ubiquitous neo-classical artwork that dominates Bangkok's galleries. There's also an underlying subtle humour in some of the figures, especially the dragons, which adds to their appeal.

Ego Clay Section 7, Soi 8
Tel: 089-499 6847

Tham Mue

Designer Wandee Jitnirat has been producing original jewellery for more than two decades and has been a Jatujak fixture for the past 16 years or so.

Given Wandee's status as a prominent activist concerned with environmental matters and the plight of stateless people and refugees in Thailand, there's a solid social context to Tham Mue. All of the products are handmade from natural materials and most of them are produced by ethnic artisans who work under fair trade conditions.

The shop sells simple brown and beige Karen textiles with jewellery produced by Mon craftswomen. Most of it is fairly heavyweight stuff, incorporating Thai silver thread and chains, polished shells embedded with more silver, roman glass and antique elements such as century-old fragments of Chinese ceramics recovered from the bed of the Chao Phraya River.

Prices range from as little as 500 baht to more than 30,000 baht for the larger pieces.

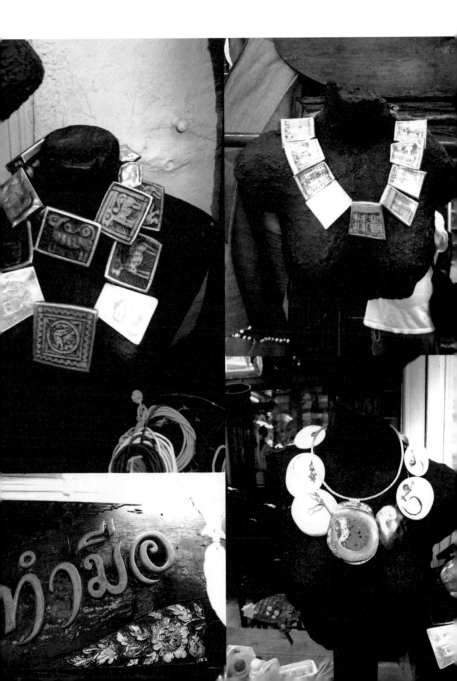

Fiendish Clothes Trap

Japanese designer Teppei Oue houses two brands under the same roof. Traps is ethnic-edged Bangkok street fashion while there is more of a Japanese flavour to Wana designs.

Teppei came up with the name Traps because he wants the clothes and the shop to "trap" customers – or at least until they make a purchase. The retro theme to many of the designs harks back to his previous incarnation as a purveyor of vintage clothing, so you can expect lurid Cuba shirts, tie-dye or Paisley-inspired 1960s geometrical patterns. Not everyone, however, will be able to pull off wearing the shorts and three-quarter length mauve or striped pants. There are also of plenty accessories on offer, including old-school digital watches, day-glo bags and cell phone holders.

Prices are very reasonable with tees costing 350 to 480 baht, shorts/pants from 650 to 980 baht and hoodies are priced from 1,000 to 1,280 baht.

Traps & Wana On the lane, section 26
Tel: 087-671 6966 Website: www.trapsbkk.com

Loaded Loafers

The boater has returned, revamped and reengineered in a way that Sonny Crocket wouldn't have dreamed possible during the 1980s heydays of Miami Vice. Russian Roulette has created its own range of the classic deck shoe, including an ankle-high variation with rolldown tartan-lined tops, in canvas, suede and buffed leather with a whole spectrum of colours including pinks, purples and greens.

You can also pick up hi-top, brogues, desert boots and loafers with the same range of colours and materials. Prices are excellent at 900 to 1,600 baht a pair.

Russian Roulette Section 4, Soi 1
Website: www.russianrouletteshoe.com

Sole Mate

AKATA is pretty much a one-stop shop for discerning women on a budget seeking shoes for any occasion. The range varies from flat-sole sandals and comfy kitten heels to lace-up stilettos and full-on spikes in glam, glitzy colours. You can customise your own pair by selecting colours from subtle tans to shocking pink, and modifying the heels with anything from sparkling beads to an imitation snakeskin finish.

AKATA Section 23, Soi 3
Tel: 081-848 1402 Website: www.akatashoes.com

Smash It Up

Couple Tos and Oil started Riotino in 2005 as a range of Asian-inspired urban wear for women who want to look good without being overly fussy. While Japanese, Taiwanese and Korean influences underpin the four labels – RIOTINO, Bobbidi, Closed-End and I SEE – the designers have put their distinctive mark on this extensive range of clothing, shoes and accessories.

RIOTINO is the flagship brand in terms of quality, and uses high-quality cottons and textiles for comfortable wear. If you're after comfortable, hassle-free workwear that is also suitable for social occasions, then browse I SEE, which is dominated by solid colours and intricate patterns. Bobbidi offers a range of mix-and-match off-the-peg items and if you're looking for something more floral (and dare one say "sweet"), then Closed-End fits the bill.

Riotino Section 3
Tel: 089-498 5098 Website: facebook.com/riotino

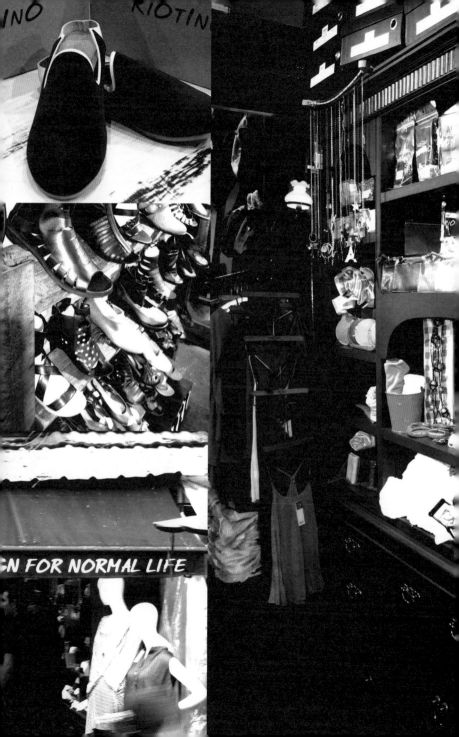

Time for Tees

Jatujak is a veritable Aladdin's Cave for T-Shirt aficionados, whether you're after vintage classics or the latest creations from some of Thailand's sharpest designers.

LineTHAI *(Tel: 089-810 1636, www.linethaitshirt.com, opposite section 17, No. 5)* tees are immediately recognisable for their iconic reworking of Thai motifs and emblems. Designs feature Buddhist and Hindu emblems and deities such as Hanuman, and *chufa* block prints printed in whites, golds, blues and a range of other colours. Despite drawing on traditional forms, there's always something contemporary about the designs, be it the use of more angular, geometric lines, or a more elongated perspective as with the Giant Swing t-shirt. Most designs are printed on black, dark blue or white tees, with some orange and mustards. Prices range from 200 to 270 baht depending on size.

If you prefer cutesy Japanese-style cartoon characters underpinned by a menacing appetite for death and destruction, then **Minitary: I'm Hardcore Breed** *(Section 4, Soi 51, Gate 23, Tel: 081-633 7782, www.minitary.tv)* is the one for you. It's tongue-in-cheek humour, day-glo colours and vector graphics all the way. **Anatomie** is a treasure trove of vintage tees, most of which are both well worn and reasonably priced. **NK 12** produces its own skate style tees with loud graphics.

UNION MALL

**GOONOO 132 YASO 134 DIM 135
NIFTY 136 My Color 137**

Young Designer Zone

Union Mall is packed full of hundreds of tiny stalls selling all forms of clothing, footwear and accessories for men and women. The Young Designer Zone on the third floor is a relatively recent addition where scores of innovative local brands can be found.

Union Mall Lad Prao Soi 1

GOONOO

Despite its name being taken from the colloquial, if not slightly raw Thai slang for "Me, You", GOONOO has a distinctly metrosexual flavour to its designs with taper-cut shirts, pinstripes and asymmetric pockets being common elements, while some of the T-shirts present a more overtly feminine look with their use of baby doll images.

GOONOO
Tel: 085-492 6494

YASO

Yaso specialises in bold, simple cotton tees and tank tops, bags and baseball caps. Most feature the YATTA! design but the collection also includes more elaborate screen prints which favour heavily contrasting colours on bright blue, yellow and orange cotton. T-shirts start from 200 baht, rising to 250 baht for metallic prints and long sleeves.

DIM

For street fashion and causal wear aimed at 17-plus and working women where simple single colours and traditional shapes dominate, check out DIM – Do It Myself. Prices range from 400 to around 3,000 baht, and while there is a good range of dresses, jean, blouses and skirts that can be worn to work or play, a few designs are reminiscent of the more gaudy influences of '80s fashion and the era of the Rah-Rah skirt.

DIM (Do It Myself)
Tel: 089-996 9171

NIFTY

While loud screen-print designs from Nifty pay homage to skate style, the shorts and denim are far too tight for any self-respecting deck head. The quality and diversity of fabric is nonetheless excellent, making this one of the new brands to look out for.

My Color

My Color specialises in hand-painted, customised baseball boots and canvas shoes for men and women. The two main styles are either flower power designs or something that features big-eyed Japanese feminine cartoon characters. Prices range from 550 to 1,200 baht and they also do made to order.

My Color
Tel: 084-145 9210 Website: www.kibkikkfashion.com

OTHER AREAS

Across the Tracks

If you've had enough of downtown Bangkok's glitzy bars and upscale shopping malls, head out to Talad Suan Rod Fai (Train Park Market), which is about half a kilometre from JJ.

Open every Saturday and Sunday from about 2pm to 1am, the market attracts a diverse range of vendors and patrons, from older Thai guys who look like they've haven't stopped rocking since the Vietnam War to modish Thais and indie kids.

The vast majority of stuff on sale are second-hand or vintage goods and you can buy everything from old dial telephones, vintage typewriters and music cassettes to tables, lamps and even parts for your customised chopper.

There are plenty of stalls selling Thai food, plus a few small bars, although many groups choose to hang out in or on the old train carriages. The best bar is Sheva Wop, a rockabilly joint run by very friendly Thais who serve beer and cocktails, plus their own Sheva Wop light rum, which is best avoided as it has an aroma similar to nail-varnish remover.

The best thing about the market is its festival-like vibe and most of the crowd seems to prefer making a nomadic trek to the boondocks to hang with their friends in a place that is cheap, cheerful and packed with creativity rather than strutting their stuff in a high-society bar.

Talad Suan Rod Fai Khampaeng Phed Road

Collectors' **Classics**

Red brick walls, antique cabinets, piles of neatly folded denim and racks of shirts crammed into various nooks and crannies recreate the look and feel of an old-school thrift store. The difference at Chaochan are the prices, as what is on offer are no run-of-the-mill second hand clothes but a select range of vintage clothing which the owner has been collecting for the past 25 years. Prices range from 800 baht up to a staggering 40,000 baht a piece, with the most collectable items (not all of which are for sale) framed on the walls alongside classic Levis adverts from the 1950s.

Added to the range of clothes and antiques are a selection of vintage Ray-Ban sunglasses brought over from Japan every three months, as well as shoes and new fashion items from Thai labels Triple-Stitch and Fragment & Fellowship.

Chaochan GF, Park Lane mall, Soi Ekkamai
Tel: 081-833 3655

J.P.HITON

Have Your Cake
and Eat It

This three-storey building contains the perfect antidote to the McDonaldisation of bookselling. Dasa Book Café is founded on a love for the printed word and the understanding that the best environment for fostering this is a place where shoppers are left alone to browse for hours on end without being pressured to buy something quickly and leave. In fact the second-hand bookstore goes far beyond just creating a welcoming atmosphere – its café is the perfect place to sit down and sample a chapter or two of a prospective book while sipping a hot cup of mocha and nibbling on a slice of chocolate cake.

The shop takes its name from the late Buddhadasa Bhikkhu, one of Thailand's most revered monks who adopted the Pali name "Dasa", which means "slave" or "servant", because "it conveys the meaning that all book lovers are 'slaves' in the sense that they can't live without books or reading," says Kaweewut, one of the owners.

Dasa Books 714/4 Sukhumvit Road
Tel: 02-661 2993 Website: www.dasabookcafe.com

Oddball Vision

Designing ugly teddy bears isn't how most people kill time at work, but for Pakinee "Ting" Rattana it provided the perfect escape from the drudgery of her job as an advertising copywriter. When the toys started to sell out at her friend's gift shop, Ting ditched her day job and opened a stall at Chatuchak market in 2005. Dreams became reality; Idealist was born and Bangkok welcomed the arrival of a new iconic product design firm.

So successful was the venture that Ting's boyfriend abandoned his career in advertising to lend support and they now have three brands: the quirky Idealist; tongue-in-cheek graphics with B-real; and the more chic Hip1101.

The duo recently opened their first stand-alone store where the full range of cuddly toys, sleeping clothes, bags, stationery and other accessories are on display.

The toys were initially aimed at kids, but it's a safe bet that these days the biggest customers are adults searching for their inner child as they pretend to be seeking out a new notepad or something similarly sensible.

Crystal Design Center
Tel: 081-646 6627 Website: www.idealistthailand.com

Nightlife

**HAIS ARE FOREVER IN SEARCH OF
ANUK (FUN).** THIS, COMBINED WITH A RELATIVELY
AISSEZ FAIRE ATTITUDE, HAS GENERATED A NIGHTLIFE
CENE OF STAGGERING PROPORTIONS. THERE ARE LITERALLY
UNDREDS OF BARS AND CLUBS DOTTED ACROSS THE CITY,
FFERING EVERYTHING FROM STREETSIDE COLD BEERS
HAT COST LITTLE MORE THAN A BOTTLE FROM THE NEARBY
-ELEVEN, TO *CHI CHI* COCKTAIL JOINTS WHICH PRICEWISE ARE
N PAR WITH THE LIKES OF NEW YORK AND LONDON.

THONG LOR ROAD IS THE EPICENTRE OF THE MORE
PSCALE BARS, SOME OF WHICH, LIKE THE IRON FAIRIES,
AVE REVOLUTIONISED THE LEVELS OF IMAGINATION AND
REATIVITY NEEDED TO ATTRACT THE ATTENTION OF THE
REA'S FICKLE YIPSTERS. OTHER VENUES, WITH THEIR
XCEPTIONAL ROOFTOP VIEWS OF THE CITYSCAPE, ARE IDEAL
OR SUNDOWNERS. AND THOSE PARTY PEOPLE WHO STILL
ARBOUR AFFECTION FOR A LESS SHOWY VIBE CAN HEAD TO
NUMBER OF BARS THAT CATER FOR THE CITY'S ALTERNATIVE
RTSY SCENE, AND WHICH, MORE OFTEN THAN NOT, TAKE A
UCH MORE LIBERAL APPROACH TO THE LICENSING LAWS.

IF YOU STILL HAVE A SONIC ITCH THAT NEEDS
CRATCHING, THEN HEAD TO BANGKOK'S MORE DISCERNING
ANCE CLUBS OR COME-AS-YOU-ARE LIVE MUSIC VENUES AND
NDULGE IN AN AUDITORY FEAST OF EVERYTHING FROM BLEEP
ND BEATS TO BLUES AND JAZZ.

BARS
Rama IV & Silom

Not a Drag

Stuck between Silom Soi 2 and Patpong, the infamous gay and straight go-go areas respectively, Silom Soi 4 attracts an up-for-it mixed crowd. It's still one of the most carefree areas with a sleaze-free street ambience. All of the bars have outside seating and it's a great place for people-watching, some of the favourites hangouts are Tapas and Noriega's. Added entertainment is provided with occasional parades and shows from the local ladyboys.

Silom Soi 4

Old School

Located in what was the original backpacker area of Bangkok before the rise of Khao San Road, Wong's Place has remained a popular late night bar since the 1980s.

Run by Sam Wong and his brother, who died in 2002, the bar is famous for its massive selection of music videos, with huge piles of VHS tapes of Top of the Pops, The Old Grey Whistle Test and other classic music programmes from the '70s and '80s piled up against the walls. There's also a continuous feed of videos playing on the plasma screen above the bar.

With a pool table upstairs, a self-service fridge stacked with Heineken, Leo, Singha and Beer Lao and occasional live music, the red-lit bar harks back to Bangkok's past as a 24-hour party city. There's no point arriving at Wong's before 11pm and, given its liberal interpretation of the licensing laws, things take a few hours to get going and it gets as tightly packed as a can of sardines. Nevertheless, it is definitely a bar that has to be experienced at least once, if not many times.

Wong's Place 27/3 Soi Sribamphen, Rama 4 Road
Tel: 081-901 0235

Sub-zero **Shooters**

As the name suggests, Minus 5 bar is an arctic temperature ice bar – one
of the only places where you can happily don a parka in Bangkok.

The cool blues of the ice and subdued lighting add to the literally chill
atmosphere of this bar where the offering is simple: 500 baht a head
for 15 minutes of unlimited Absolut vodka shots (diluted with fruit juice)
served in glasses made from ice.

Minus5 Bar
Tel: 02-238 4300 Website: www.minus5bangkok.com

BARS
Sukhumvit Road

Kicks like a Mule

While it may not feature the quirky interiors of some of the city's newer cocktail bars, in many ways Hyde & Seek Gastro Bar offers the best overall experience. Created by a team that includes a Thai celebrity chef, a bunch of self-confessed "Swedish bar nerds" and an interior designer turned cocktail expert, the Manhattan-style bar is a creative hub of devilish drinks.

The massive open bar is as much a source of entertainment as a place to hang out. When it gets busy you can watch the mixologists at work as they crank out a staggering range of drinks from Cosmopolitans and Long Island Ice Teas to more creative cocktails such as the Hemmingway Daiquiri or a Horse's Neck.

Drinks are served in a range of vessels, from hi-ball glasses to jam jars and copper cups, and Hyde & Seek offers what may well be the world's biggest mojito – the massive 50cm-tall glasses hold ten cocktails.

The drinks list includes 28 tequilas, more than 30 vodkas, 26-plus rums and over 80 wines. The chef takes his own contemporary take on classic London and New York pub dinners, with the brunch being one of the key draws, especially if you're hung over.

Hyde & Seek Gastro Bar 65/1 Athenee Residence, Soi Ruamrudee
Website: www.hydeandseek.com
Daily 11am–1am

Sweet and Simple

Since it's origins in 1983, Cheap Charlie's has been pulling a crowd of dedicated drinkers who are enamoured with its simple no-frills offering of street-side standing room with a few tables and stools.

When the eponymous Charlie passed away, his brother Sathit took up the helm and he now works the wooden contraption that stands for the bar with a couple of staff.

The bar itself is something of a cross between a Wild West saloon and a barnacle-encrusted ship hull, with a buffalo skull, a turtle shell and other dead and desiccated remains tacked on to the structure; along with the odd spiritual phallus and other arcane knick-knacks. Maybe it's really a shrine to the great god Bacchus where locals leave their offerings.

Despite it's decidedly down-at-heel offering, Cheap Charlie's is patronised by a diverse crowd of locals, many of whom use it as a meeting spot before hitting the clubs further down Soi 11.

Cheap Charlie's Soi Sukhumvit 11/1, Khlong Toei Nuae 10110
Take the first left when heading down Soi 11 from Sukhumvit Road.

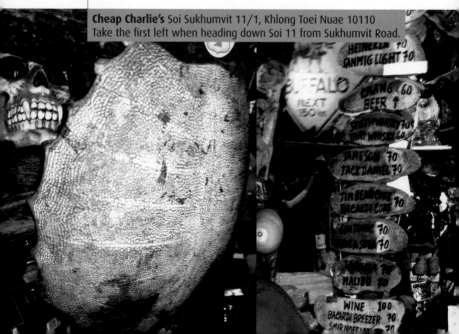

Apathy **Rules**

Mongkol Sanla is brutally honest about why he set up Bar 23 a few years ago. "I like drinking... and all the bars and places that I went to weren't my style, so I opened my own place. Oh, and we're closed on Sundays and Mondays because basically I'm lazy and want to stay home and watch movies."

This lackadaisical tone clearly strikes a chord with a certain Bangkok demographic – many of the regulars are local journalists, UN workers, English teachers, younger Japanese expats and, of course, Sanla's friends.

There's a living room appeal to the interiors, which are tastefully and minimally decked out with comfy seats, display cabinets and a vintage fridge, and artwork – including Mongkol's own paintings – hangs on the walls.

The Macbook on the bar is a treasure trove of classic tracks, so expect anything from The Smiths and Echobelly to Thai electronica from Miraculous.

Bar 23 Sukhumvit Soi 23
Tel: 081-264 4471

Class Act

While located near to the Thong Lor/Ekamai yipster ghetto, WTF (which stands for "Wonderful Thai Friends", allegedly) definitely boasts regulars with an identity of their own. The converted shop house has a gallery upstairs, with the brightly-painted ground floor as the bar area which is decorated with classic Thai album covers and photos by owner Chris Wise, a photojournalist, and his artist wife Som.

The food is Thai-style tapas and bite-sized snacks, plus a great range of sprits and some imaginative cocktails – including a beer mojito, which tastes a lot better than it sounds.

The place is packed on Fridays and Saturdays when the crowds spill out onto the street, but it's always a good place to meet interesting people and it's a popular hangout for artists, journalists and musicians, especially leftfield expats who have lived in Bangkok for several years.

Another plus is the music policy that ensures a constant stream of great tunes, be it from a regular deejay or a live band. Som and Chris recently opened OPPOSITE, a social art space in the building across the road which hosts exhibitions, film screenings and other events.

WTF
Tel: 02-662 6246 Website: www.wtfbangkok.com
Closed Mondays

BARS
Thong Lor

A Rum Time

Dark wood interiors and gilded windows, the sills of which are oddly enough stacked with jars of pickled onions, dominate this New York-style saloon where a four-piece blues band plays every night, crammed into an unfeasibly small space. It's just on the right side of claustrophobic, but then Fat Gut'z seeks to conjure the vibe of a 1920s speakeasy.

The two-floor bar is another Ashley Sutton creation and while its concept is radically different from The Iron Fairies, there's the same trademark attention to detail and imagination. Positioned as a fish and chips bar that serves rum and whisky, you can expect a range of cocktails that still pack a mighty punch.

Fat Gut'z Grass Thong Lor
Tel: 02-714 9832 Website: www.fatgutz.com

The Iron Fairies

There's something of a Terry Gilliam weirdness to the interior of The Iron Fairies, which is packed full of antique shelving, glass bottles of fairy dust and dark nooks and crannies to hide away in. Perhaps this comes as no surprise as the bar is based on a dream and a graphic novel penned by Aussie native Ashley Sutton – you can actually purchase iron fairies which he has cast himself.

This ethereal journey continues as you move upstairs where classic black-and-white silent movies are projected onto the black and exposed brick walls. The in-house jazz band sits next to a cast iron spiral staircase, which doubles as a stage for a ballgown-clad vocalist who adds a hint of the bordello to the otherwise Alice-in-Wonderland aesthetic.

When Sutton opened the bar in 2010 he started something a revolution in the way people drink; raising the bar in terms of the amount of imagination a venue must have to attract the current hip crowd. Things have moved away from bottles of Black Label to a range of perfectly-mixed strong cocktails (the Dirty Martinis are excellent). The food has its own twist too, with burgers served pinned to wooden boards with a steak knife.

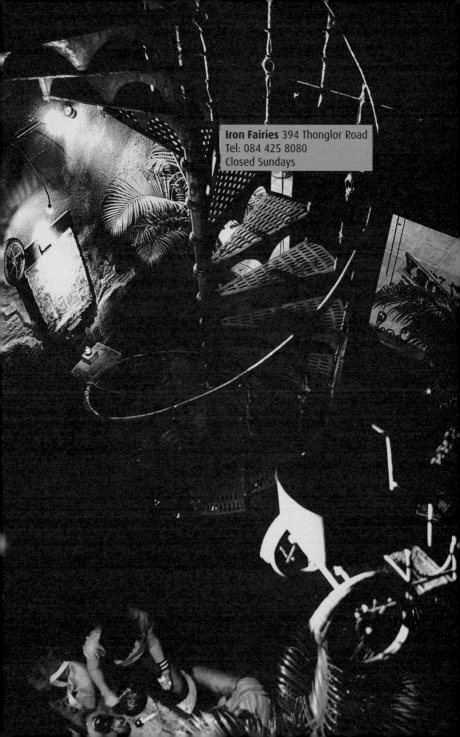

Iron Fairies 394 Thonglor Road
Tel: 084 425 8080
Closed Sundays

Plastic Fantastic

As the third instalment in Ashley Sutton's trilogy of mentalist cocktail bars, Clouds casts its eye on an eco-friendly future, or at least that's what the design supposedly hints at. Transparent acrylic counters are embedded with skeletal leaves, walls are decked in water bottles, a cloud machine cranks continuously, silver baubles and Barbie dolls hang suspended from the ceiling and a tree encapsulated in a Perspex cubicle is the focal point of the room. A gas-fired oven in which the staff bake artisan pizzas flames away behind the bar from where wine and vodka cocktails are served. Be sure to try the signature Cloud 9, a wonderfully sour mix concocted from a dragon fruit base.

Overall, Clouds is full of imagination, although some elements are a little bit too pompous – the reserved signs marked for "Prius drivers" and the kimono-clad woman sitting on a pedestal knitting go beyond what can be excused as post-modern irony.

Clouds Seenspace, Thong Lor Soi 13
Tel: 02-185 2368

Hop-head Heaven

For years, beer drinkers in Thailand were consigned to a paltry mix of brews that barely extended beyond Chang, Singha, Heineken, Tiger and the odd premium import such as Guinness and Tetley's.

Fortunately, for the past four years Chris Foo has been waging war on this woeful situation with House of Beers, or HOBS as it's better known, which first opened its doors at Penny's Balcony (there are now four outlets in Bangkok). The Belgian pub and bistro offers a range of 22 Belgian brews that range from a mild cherry beer to the heady tripelbock.

Red brick walls adorned with stained glass give something of a medieval Flemish feel to the place, adding to the urge to quaff flagons of ale while eating mussels and chomping on the double-fried crunchy Belgian fries, which are served with garlic mayonnaise.

House of Beers Penny's Balcony, Soi Thong Lor
Tel: 02-392 5313 Website: www.hobsbkk.com

Brazen Bossanova

There's an industrial feel to the polished concrete and brick interiors at She Bar, but once the place fills up there's a much warmer, friendlier buzz than you may have first expected.

While the venue attracts its fair share of 20-somethings shod in Prada heels and clutching Gucci bags, there's enough of an older crowd to balance things out. The bar serves a wide range of cocktails, plus some decent beers including Schneider Weisse, Bacchus and draft Stowford Press cider. But the main thing that sets it apart is the live music – it's one of the only places in town where you can indulge in live Bossanova.

She Bar Penny's Balcony, Soi Thong Lor
Tel: 02-714 7642

Hallelujah

With members of Modern Dog –
one of Thailand's oldest and most
successful indie bands – being
partners in Happy Monday, it comes as no surprise
that this small bar on the corner of Ekamai Soi 10 has become something
of a Mecca for music-conscious Thais.

The interiors are pretty stark with white painted walls and exposed
brick, but this makes the shelves of vinyl (that's the stuff that preceded
MP3s and compact discs) stand out all the more. There's a refreshing
burst of nostalgia from the selection of 12" LPs from the likes of Blondie,
Depeche Mode, The Clash and, of course, The Happy Mondays.

Most people choose to sit outside where the music plays through a
sound system, and with different deejays every night the range of tunes
is pretty diverse, from The Cure and Radiohead to the latest releases from
Small Room Records, an alternative label whose studio is located just
round the corner.

Happy Monday Ekamai Soi 10
Tel: 02-714 3935

Great with Mates

Shop by day, bar by night, the interior at Tuba is a cross between an antique store and a bric-a-brac shop. The collection of goods ranges from art deco lamps and a life-size model of Superman to psychedelic lamps and kids' toys. Apparently everything can be purchased, but it's unlikely that you'll ever see a bunch of inebriated revellers lugging a leopard skin *chaise longue* down the road at 1am after a hard night of drinking.

Tuba's layout makes it a great place to hang out with mates; there are plenty of secluded and cornered-off places to sit on the two floors, although this makes it less than ideal for mingling. Thai and Italian food is on offer till the early hours and the ubiquitous range of lager is complemented with a few weisse beers, but the place is known for its legendary margaritas of gargantuan proportions.

Tube Design Furniture Soi Ekkamai 21
Tel: 02-711 5500 Website: www.design-athome.com

Hipster Haven

Tucked away deep down Soi 2 is a haven of laidback left-field cool that offers a stark contrast to the swanky bars and bistros that have sprung up elsewhere in the Ekamai and Thong Lor area.

Bangkok Bar, complete with its retro-inspired interiors and '70s-style sofas that Grandpa would have loved, serves cold beers and cocktails to a predominantly laid-back Thai crowd.

If you're peckish, there's a great range of Thai food, the best of which are the beer snacks such as *moo daet diaow* (deep-fried sun dried pork) and *yum takrai* (spicy lemongrass salad). The music ranges from guitar to electronica and there are live bands on Wednesday and Fridays.

If you're more inclined towards a chat with friends, make a bee-line for the leafy courtyard out back.

Bangkok Bar Ekamai Soi 2
Tel: 02-714 0531

BARS
Thonburi

Way out West

Kudos, a few hundred metres before Sura Bar, is a much grander affair. The two-storey venue complete with club and rooftop terrace has proven that large-scale massage parlours are not the only entertainment centres that can make it as suburban destination venues.

While the joint boasts a massive menu, a solid drinks list and acoustic music, it has started to make a name for itself by bringing in fairly heavyweight Thai bands such as Blah Blah, Jetsetter and Scrubb. It's definitely worth checking out if you're over this side of town, but things can be a bit quiet if there's no band playing.

Kudos 249 Ratchapruek Rd
Tel: 02-57 8094 Website: www.kudosclub.net
Open daily, 6pm–4am

Head to the Beach

Heading out to the back of Bangkok's west side, better known as Thonburi, is no mean feat – the Skytrain doesn't yet extend all the way and taxi drivers are no masters of navigation. However, if you do decide to throw caution to the wind and cross the Chao Phraya River, then be sure to check out Sura Bar Party, Bangkok's only beach bar.

This small bar has proven to be a huge hit with former and current students from the nearby Siam University as well as over-30s living on this side of the river. The design is big on imagination and low on budget with its covered bar, sail-type tarpaulin roofing, deck chairs and plenty of sand... there's even a speed boat and a few palm trees thrown in for good measure.

Live music plays every night, with two sets on Fridays and Saturdays, and music ranging from acoustic and folk to more upbeat Thai ska.

There's no pretense or attitude at Sura Bar Party and it is always busy. It opens from about 6pm, but you'll need to reserve a table on most nights from 7.30pm onwards.

Sura Bar Party 317/1 Ratchapruek Road
Tel: 085-188 6131

BARS
Rooftop Bangkok

Aerial Schmooze

There's always been something of a tussle over who's the best between Sirocco and Vertigo, Bangkok's first two high-altitude bars. While both have their strengths and weaknesses, and they are some of, if not the best places to enjoy Bangkok's technicolour sunsets, Sirocco wins out overall.

Situated on the top of the State Tower, this restaurant/bar is on the circuit of must-visit Bangkok venues. The steps down to the main bar area are enough to give many people vertigo, with the transparent perspex barrier adding to the feeling of giddy exposure, but the perch offers a truly awesome view of Bangkok's cityscape, the Chaophraya River and Thonburi. There's live jazz every night and a reasonable range of cocktails and wines to choose from, although it may be best to taste the wine first to ensure you're getting a fresh pour.

Vertigo was the first party in town when it opened on the roof of The Banyan Tree hotel. Located further up Sathorn Road, it offers a better view of inner Bangkok and Lumpini Park, although you miss out on the river view. It does offer a 360-degree scenic view and you feel more exposed to the elements, which can be quite fun. However, there's no live music and the bar is more crowded with less space to walk around compared to Sirocco.

Both venues have strict dress codes so do check ahead before going.

Vertigo & Moon Bar The Banyan Tree, Sathorn Road
Tel: 02-679 1200 Website: www.banyantree.com

Sirocco State Tower, Silom Road
Tel: 02-624 9555 Website: www.lebua.com

Three Sixty Lounge

As the only high-altitude bar on the west bank of the Chaopraya River,
Three Sixty Lounge affords a unique view of the city in all directions. The
enclosed bar's subdued interiors and candlelit lighting make it ideal for a
romantic night out, but it also has a good reputation for live jazz and it's
one of the few such venues with lounge-style seating, making it a top
spot for settling in for the night. The fact that it's not open-air makes it a
popular year-round destination.

Three Sixty Lounge Millennium Hilton Bangkok, 123 Charoen Nakhon Road
Tel: 02-442 2000 Website: www.bangkok.hilton.com

Golden Views

Unlike the polished perfection at the city's upscale rooftop bars, Pranakorn Bar & Gallery is a what-you-see-is-what-you-get kind of place. For 12 years it has been a key alternative hangout and a favourite for art students from the nearby Silpakorn University.

The four-storey building has a cafe on the ground floor, a small art gallery with a pool table on the second and a bar on the level above. However, it's the rooftop terrace that has the greatest appeal with its unspoilt view of Wat Phu Khao Tong or the Golden Mount, which towers above the cityscape at night in all its gilded glory.

As you may expect, the music selection is as varied as the artists who frequent the place, with tunes ranging from jazz and blues to indie rock, so don't be surprised to hear songs by Burt Bacharach and The Smiths playing back to back.

Pranakorn Bar & Gallery 58/2 Soi Damnoen Klang Tai, Ratchadamnoen Klang Road
Tel: 02-622 0282

Nest

Given its location on one of Bangkok's biggest clubbing streets, Nest attracts a different crowd from the other sky bars. There's a strong contingent of youthful Thais, Indians and former international school students, as well as locals getting ready to hit the nearby nightspots.

Nest Le Fenix Hotel, Sukhumvit Soi 11
Tel: 02-255 0638 Website: www.thenestbangkok.com

The bar takes its name from the rattan nest-like day beds that are dotted around the terrace. They're great if you turn up for a snuggle with your significant other, but if you're out with friends it's probably better to opt for a normal table. There's a decent range of cocktails and beers, even if they're somewhat overpriced. Nonetheless, Nest has decent local live music from Britpop-style bands as well as monthly parties and regular deejay sets. The lineups are posted on the website.

Secluded Space

Named after the owner's love of the amber nectar, Barley Bar & Bistro is a stone's throw from the frenzy that is Silom Road. The two-level venue includes a darkly-lit enclosed bar and a rooftop terrace and it's a good place if you fancy an open-air bar which isn't ridiculously busy, or need to escape from the more hectic nightlife on Silom Soi 4. The live band adds to the chilled vibe and mainly plays down-tempo pop, jazz and soul.

Barley Bar & Bistro Silom Food Channel between Silom Soi 5 & 7
Tel: 087-033 3919 Website: www.barleybistro.com

Jam Session

When it opened its doors about a decade ago, Adhere's simple offering of a small intimate bar with live music every night was a hit with lovers of stripped back blues. Georgia, a larger-than-life Thai singer with a voice reminiscent of Janis Joplin, was one of the key attractions back in the day and she still drops in to perform on occasion, while all-Thai band Bangkok Connection plays most nights.

There are normally two live sets a night and they are always good. Most of the bands have been performing together for years, so the performances are tight and, more often than not, the first set which kicks off at 8.30pm resembles more of an impromptu jam session than anything else.

Despite the fact that this small bar is packed every night with a mix of fiercely loyal Thai and expat locals, many of whom are musicians, it remains a friendly and inviting venue that is refreshingly free of cliques. Due to the size, it's worth arriving early if you want a seat.

Adhere The 13th Blues Bar 13 Samsen Road
Tel: 089-769 4613

Sound City

It's a decent trek across the city to get to Parking Toys, so it's best to either turn up late or get there early enough to occupy a sofa or two and settle in for the night. If you like unpretentious, laid-back venues, then this one of the best gig spots in the city and its appeal centres around retro interiors, the easygoing vibe of the locals and a solid alternative music policy. The end result is akin to chilling out at a friend's house with the privilege of having hi-energy bands playing live in the living room.

The bands are pretty diverse, but the music is mostly guitar-based alternative or indie rock. Mahajamreon, the bar's own band, blends blues, punk rock, Thai ska and electronica, with fun being the emphasis of every set.

More recently, a number of international bands such as Evaline from California have stopped off to play at Parking Toys when they're passing through town.

Parking Toys Soi Mai-laap, Rahmintra 14
Tel: 02-907 2228

NIGHTCLUBBING
Clubs

Egalitarian Electronica

Café by day, club by night, no other Bangkok nightspot offers such a tremendous vista of the city's historical heart, but truth be told, partygoers at Café Democ are typically too entranced by the bleeps and beats being played out to ponder the glorious view of Democracy Monument from the art deco windows.

Over time, most clubs either fall by the wayside due to the fickle nature of the nightlife scene, that or they lose their edge and become too commercial. Democ has successfully avoided that despite spinning tunes for a decade or so. Its dedication to giving the punters what they want – the club is passionate about drum 'n' bass, breakbeat culture, acid and tech house, with tracks laid down by international deejays and leading Thai turntablists – is balanced by introducing new sounds and keeping the music policy diverse with a rotation of soul, funk and indie nights.

Cafe Democ Ratchadamnoen Rd
Tel: 02-622 2572

Never get Bored

Club Culture attracts a similar crowd to Café Democ, although the three-room venue has a much larger capacity and on any night you can follow your musical fancy and check out out dubstep, electro and rock as you make your way around the different spaces.

There's also a martini bar if you fancy giving your ears a break from the beats.

Few other venues offer such a mix of sounds under the same roof, and to be honest, most of the other sizable venues tend to be much more commercial, an accusation you could never level at Club Culture.

The range of promoters and in-house nights is unsurpassed in Bangkok and ranges from funk, rare groove and soul, to Brazilian salsa, tech house and trance. To spice things up there are also a number of regular theme nights, such as ABC [Anything But Clothes] where revelers are encouraged to take a DIY approach to their attire using anything from beer crates to tin foil.

Club Culture Ratchadamnoen Klang Road
Tel: 089-497 8422 Website: www.club-culture-bkk.com

LED

NIGHTCLUB - BANGKOK

Given that the team behind LED have brought in the likes of deejays Tiesto, Armin van Buuren and Boy George to play in Bangkok, you may expect the entry price to Bangkok's newest club to be pretty steep. However, despite having a massive sound system, mind-bending light shows and what they claim is the largest LED screen in any club in the capital, you currently don't need to spend a dime to get in.

But it won't be the free entry and some of the most reasonably-priced drinks for any dance club in Bangkok that bring you through the doors, it will be the music. Fridays is Urban Music with hip hop and R&B, and on Saturdays it's electro sounds all the way with an up-for-it crowd each night.

LED Royal City Avenue
Tel: 086-860 0808 Website: www.facebook.com/LEDclub

Q Bar

Q Bar was the catalyst that transformed Sukhumvit Soi 11 from a sleepy suburban side street into one of the city's main clubbing streets. It was also the first destination club to branch away from the cavernous Thai-style warehouses to a cutting-edge designed venue that attracts international legends such as Ice T, Afrika Islam and Carl Cox.

For 12 years it has been satisfying Bangkok's clubbing community with its combination of a sophisticated venue, sets from top local and international deejays and strong drinks.

It continues to pull the crowds with well-established regular nights that include Block Party Wednesdays where Sum-1 and DJ Toru play hip hop and old skool, and Bangers & Mashups on Saturdays with DJ Octo and Travellin' Matt playing everything from house and heavy beats to trance.

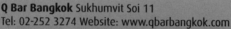

Q Bar Bangkok Sukhumvit Soi 11
Tel: 02-252 3274 Website: www.qbarbangkok.com

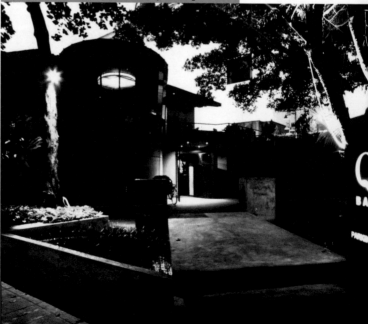

Bed in for the Night

Simply put, Bed Supperclub has been Bangkok's leading clubbing destination for locals and tourists ever since the white two-room torpedo-like venue opened its doors in 2002.

Apart from its extravagant design, the foundation of the bright, split-level interiors are the oversized beds from which the club takes its name – they cannot be beaten for comfort and no other club has quite the same lounging appeal.

Residents mix up the sounds at the Bar and in the White Room on a number of regular nights with tunes from deejays Freddy Garcia, Fred Jungo and Eddy Frampton. There's everything from Afro beats and funk to deep house, acid and dubstep. A host of international names fly in to grace the decks, including Kraftykuts, Goldie, Norman Jay and Laurent Garnier. But regardless of who's playing at Bed, you're always guaranteed a top night out.

Bed Supperclub Sukhumvit Soi 11
Tel: 02-651 3537 Website: www.bedsupperclub.com

Underground Sounds

For a change from the more upscale nightspots, head to Glow – a small, three-floor club with a more underground appeal than the likes of Bed and Q Bar.

Most of the action here takes place on the main floor near the glowing bar and music is provided by an entourage of predominantly Thai deejays with a penchant for tech house and electro.

One of the key attractions at Glow, which is in part down to its small, cozy size, is the local feel to the place. A regular crowd turns up to hang out at the bar most nights before the place starts to fill up, injecting a more personable vibe to the party atmosphere than at some of the larger clubs.

Glow Sukhumvit Soi 23
Website: www.glowbkk.com

Dance Dungeon

It's hard to think of a cooler venue in Bangkok than Blue Velvet. Designed by the team behind Mansion7 (see p74), nowhere else can beat the pure strangeness of this bar-cum-club which is the only medieval castle in the city.

Once you pass through the main portcullis you enter a granite-walled interior with chessboard tiled floors and a dark wooden bar, and suspended from the ceiling are scores of oversized light bulbs that echo the cover of Pink Floyd's *Delicate Sound of Thunder*. There are plenty of cubbyholes and hideaways furnished with comfy sofas and Chesterfield chairs. It's a great place to wander about with little tunnels and winding staircases to explore.

The music varies night by night, but the deejays generally play more mellow sounds than banging tunes to suit the club's lounge vibe. The crowd is predominantly party-mad hi-so Thais and the atmosphere can be quite cliquey, but it's easy enough to ignore the pretense if you turn up with your own group.

Blue Velvet Thonglor Soi 5
Tel: 02-392 1769

Overnight

CHOOSING WHERE TO STAY IN A CITY WHICH IS FAMOUS FOR ITS SERVICE AND HOSPITALITY AND BOASTS THOUSANDS OF HOTELS IS NO MEAN FEAT. WHILE BANGKOK IS HOME TO A HOST OF GLOBAL BRANDS AND RESORTS, SOME OF THE MOST ENJOYABLE STAYS ARE TO BE HAD AT THE MORE INDIVIDUAL, SMALLER HOTELS.

THE FOLLOWING PROPERTIES HAVE BEEN SELECTED BECAUSE THEY OFFER SOMETHING UNIQUE; BE IT THEIR DESIGN, HISTORY OR RANGE OF SERVICES. ALL OF THEM PROVIDE A PERSONAL TOUCH THAT CANNOT BE FOUND IN LARGER CORPORATE HOTELS OR BUDGET HOSTELS. THAT BEING SAID, QUALITY AND VALUE MAKE THE BEST OF BEDFELLOWS IN BANGKOK AND THERE'S NO NEED TO BREAK THE BANK TO PAY FOR AN OVERNIGHT STAY.

A Family Affair

There's a very personal touch to just about everything at the Old Bangkok Inn, which has ten bespoke rooms, each with its own individual Thai floral theme of scents and colours – such as lemongrass, lotus and jasmine. Set in the heart of the city's historic Ratanakosin Island district, the property is located on the site of a former palace owned by the Tulyanond family who now operate the hotel.

It was renovated in 2005 with the aim of reducing the property's impact on the environment by using reclaimed wood and installing solar heating (a portion of the room fees is also donated to a community support project). But the bedrock of the Inn's first class service is Nantiya, the owner, who prepares breakfast each day, offers travel advice and, in her own words, "always try my best to personally give each and every guest all the time and attention I have."

Room prices start at $92 per night.

Old Bangkok Inn 607 Pra Sumen Road
Tel: 02-629 1787 Website: www.oldbangkokinn.com

Nice and Slow

Phranakorn-Nornlen indisputably takes one of the most distinctive and imaginative approaches to providing a unique experience while staying in Bangkok.

It's the perfect place to step out of stress and enjoy life at a slower, more relaxed pace. There are no televisions, jabbering away on mobile phones is frowned upon and the child-friendly hotel wears its environmental heart on its sleeve – the property boasts a lush, green space for guests to relax in, serves vegetables grown on its organic rooftop garden and has a range of eco-friendly homemade spa products for sale in its shop.

There's also a special play area for the little ones and the property runs a number of street-level tours for guests wanting a more immersive experience of Thai culture.

Phranakorn-Nornlen Boutique Hotel 46 Thewet Soi 1
Tel: 02-628 8188 Website: www.phranakorn-nornlen.com

Good Sleep, Nice Price

Lub D, pronounced "laap dee", which is Thai for a good night's sleep, is probably one of the city's coolest hostels (or pair of hostels). A far cry from the sweaty dorms that are too often the experience for people travelling on a budget, Lub D offers contemporary design, friendly service, nice prices and decent beds in two prime central locations.

Design at the Silom hostel is inspired by a map of Bangkok with cartographic elements and street signs used throughout the property, while the location is ideal for checking out the city's renowned nightlife.

Those seeking retail therapy should stay at the Lub D Siam Square, which is close to the major malls and shopping districts.

Both locations offer a range of rooms from dorms to deluxe doubles. There's free Wi-Fi throughout, a decent bar and purpose-built communal areas that aim to create a friendly, inclusive environment.

Lub D Silom Decho Road
Tel: 02-634 7999

Lub D Siam Rama 1 Road
Tel: 02-612 4999
Website: www.lubd.com

Chinois Chic

Despite its reputation for having the best produce, biggest fruits and freshest seafood available in Bangkok, Chinatown (Yaowarat) is home to very few decent hotels. This makes Shanghai Mansion stand out all the more for its 1930s Chinois classicism and fabulously detailed design.

The mansion is located in a nine-storey building, which was one of the highest in the area when it was built in 1892. The interiors, which are decorated with Chinese antiques and classical elements, such as black-and-white chessboard tiles, evoke the wonders of a bygone era. Additional facilities include a Chinese water garden and Cotton, a jazz bar with a fast growing reputation for live music.

Shanghai Mansion 479-481 Yaowaraj Road, Tel: 02-221 2121 Website: www.shanghaimansion.com

A Room a Day

With just six guest rooms, Seven is one of the smallest hotels in Bangkok and it certainly has one of the most personal approaches.

The boutique hotel combines distinctive mix of Thai art and culture, and the fact that the kingdom is the only country in the world which designates a specific colour for each day of the week – Monday is yellow, Tuesday is pink, Wednesday is green, Thursday is orange, Friday is blue, Saturday is purple and Sunday is red. Each of the rooms is based on this theme, with colours and artwork to match the tradition, and 7th Heaven combining a gallery, reception and bar.

It's hard to find a smaller, more intimate place to stay in the city. Better still, the hotel provides guests with complimentary mobile phones preloaded with numbers for the owner Jane Sanguanpiyapand's personal recommendations for restaurants, shops, bars and spas.

Rooms range from 2,990 to 5,490 baht.

Seven 3/15 Sawasdee 1, Sukhumvit 31
Tel: 02-662 0951 Website: www.sleepatseven.com

ACKNOWLEDGEMENTS

First and foremost, profuse thanks and apologies must be directed to my lovely wife Mint and our three-year old daughter Isabel. Not only have they been a bedrock, they have tolerated numerous family days out being transformed into research trips for *Cool Bangkok!*, where many a nice lunch or trip to the shops ended up as harebrained dashes across town to check out new boutiques and cafes – which more often than not turned out to be damp squibs rather than the next best thing. Beyond that, they have put up with me being annoying and irritable during the all-consuming act of writing the book and only griefed me for my outbursts half of the time.

Thanks must also go to the team at Marshall Cavendish, who have done a great job in designing the book, with a special mention for my editors Melvin Neo and Stephanie Yeo, whose Zen-like patience has kept the project on course.

I must also tip my hat to some of the best sources of information on what do to in the city, most notably Karla Cripps and the team at CNNGO.com, Mason Florence and Max Crosbie-Jones at *Bangkok 101* magazine (www.bangkok101.com), *BK Magazine* (bk.asia-city.com), and last but not least, Chris Mitchell at TravelHappy.info, who introduced me to what has become my favourite café in the city, Bitter Brown.

Cool!

Bangkok

Editor: Stephanie Yeo
Designer: Steven Tan

All photos provided by the author except pages 58, 67–69, 148–149 by Rose Cracknell and page 107 by Nana Chen. Additional images courtesy of Footmaster, Panpuri Organic Spa, The Reading Room, House RCA, Kathmandu Photo Gallery, Serindia Gallery, Stephff's Gallery, TCDC, Pedalicious Bike & Bistro, Edoya, La Table de Tee, Café Ice, nahm, Face, La Monita, The Seafood Bar, Xuan Mai, Soul Food Mahanakorn, Serenade, Sra Bua, Gaggan, Somtumized, Bangkok Bagel Bakery, THANN Café, Sugar Lust, Secret Weapon, VII Athletic Club, Eco Shop, Kan'ser, wwa, Greyhound, 10,000 Miles Through the Himalayas, Painkiller, Phil, Noxx, JBB", Karmakamet, Traps & Wana, Riotino, Dasa, Idealist, Hyde & Seek, WTF, The Iron Fairies, HOBS, Kudos, The Banyan Tree, Sirroco, Millennium Hilton Bangkok, Nest, Barley Bar & Bistro, Club Culture, LED, Q Bar, Bed Supperclub, Glow, Old Bangkok Inn, Phranakorn-Nornlen Boutique Hotel, Lub D, Shanghai Mansion and Seven.

© 2012 Marshall Cavendish International
Published by Marshall Cavendish Editions
An imprint of Marshall Cavendish International
1 New Industrial Road, Singapore 536196

This publication represents the opinions and views of the author based on her personal experience, knowledge and research. The author and publisher have used their best efforts in preparing this book and disclaim liability rising directly and indirectly from the use and application of this book.

Other Marshall Cavendish Offices:
Marshall Cavendish Ltd. 5th Floor, 32-38 Saffron Hill, London EC1N 8 FH, UK • Marshall Cavendish Corporation. 99 White Plains Road, Tarrytown NY 10591-90 USA • Marshall Cavendish International (Thailand) Co Ltd. 253 Asoke, 12th Flr, Sukhumvit 21 Road, Klongtoey Nua, Wattana, Bangkok 10110, Thailand • Marshall Cavendish (Malaysia) Sdn Bhd, Times Subang, Lot 46, Subang Hi-Tec Industrial Park, Batu Tiga, 40000 Shah Alam, Selangor Darul Ehsan, Malaysia

Marshall Cavendish is a trademark of Times Publishing Limited

National Library Board Singapore Cataloguing-in-Publication Data

Lowe, Greg, 1974-
Cool! Bangkok : your essential guide to what's hip & happening / Greg Lowe. – Singapore : Marshall Cavendish Editions, c2011.
p. cm.
ISBN : 978-981-2618-74-0 (pbk.)

1. Bangkok (Thailand) – Guidebooks. I. Title.

DS589.B2   OCN745221706
915.9304 — dc22

Printed in Singapore by KWF Printing Pte Ltd